Mathematical Understanding 5–11

A Practical Guide to Creative Communication
in Mathematics

Mathematical Understanding 5–11

A Practical Guide to Creative Communication in Mathematics

Edited by Anne D. Cockburn

P·C·P

Paul Chapman Publishing

Paul Chapman Publishing
A SAGE Publications Company
1 Oliver's Yard
55 City Road
London EC1Y 1SP

SAGE Publications Inc.
2455 Teller Road
Thousand Oaks, California 91320

SAGE Publications India Pvt Ltd
B1/I1 Mohan Cooperative Industrial Area
Mathura Road, Post Bag 7
New Delhi 110 044

SAGE Publications Asia-Pacific Pte Ltd
33 Pekin Street # 02-01
Far East Square
Singapore 048763

Library of Congress Control Number: 2006940627

A catalogue record for this book is available from the British Library

ISBN- 978-1-4129-4505-9
ISBN- 978-1-4129-4506-6 (pbk)

Typeset by Pantek Arts Ltd, Maidstone, Kent
Printed in Great Britain by Cromwell Press Ltd, Trowbridge Wiltshire
Printed on paper from sustainable resources

Contents

About the Authors

Anne Cockburn was born and raised in Edinburgh. Following a degree in psychology at the University of St Andrews, she qualified as a primary teacher at Moray House (Edinburgh). She taught in Scotland before moving south of the border to undertake her doctoral studies in early years mathematics education. Her books include *Understanding the Mathematics Teacher: A Study of Practice in the First School* (with Desforges, 1987), *Understanding Mathematics in the Lower Primary Years* (with Haylock, 1997, 2003, 2007) and *Teaching Mathematics with Insight* (1999). She is currently a Reader in Education at the University of East Anglia, Norwich.

Milan Hejný was born in Martin (Slovakia). He graduated from Charles University, Prague, Faculty of Mathematics and Physics. He taught geometry and topology at several universities including Prague and Bratislava. He then transferred to mathematics education. His main publications include *Sixteen Mathematical Stories* (with Niepel, 1983), which presents mathematics in fairy tale contexts; *Theory of Mathematics Education* (1990), which is the main textbook used for teacher education in the Czech Republic and Slovakia; *The Child, School and Mathematics* (with Kuřina, 2001), which analyses different methods of enhancing pupils' mathematical culture. He is a professor of mathematics and mathematics education at Charles University, Faculty of Education.

Diana Hunscheidt was born in Oldenburg, Germany. After studying mathematics and arts at Carl von Ossietzky of Oldenburg, she qualified as a teacher and taught at a primary school in a small town near Bremen. She is currently working at Carl von Ossietzky University as a lecturer of pre-service teachers. She has recently started a PhD, focusing on children's strategies when using BlockCAD (virtual Lego software).

Alan Pagden grew up in Southern Africa. He studied Developmental Psychology at the University of Sussex and completed a Masters in Education with the Open University. He is currently studying for a PhD at the University of Bristol under the supervision of Professor Martin Hughes. After teaching in several different mainstream and special schools in the UK and abroad, he worked for a number of years in initial teacher training and with practising teachers at the University of East Anglia where he is currently a Research Associate. His main research interest is in ICT and learning, in particular the possibilities afforded by virtually augmented spaces in the domain of children's geographies. He teaches on the MA programme for international students delivering a module on 'multigrade teaching'.

Andrea Peter-Koop was born and raised in Bielefeld, Germany. Following a degree in primary teacher training at the University of Bielefeld, she moved to Melbourne to undertake her doctoral studies at the Australian Catholic University, investigating mathematics teachers professional learning processes. Back in Germany she took up a position at the University of Münster where she conducted a three-year study on primary students' collaborative problem solving and modelling strategies. She is the editor of the international *Mathematics Teacher Education Series* published by Springer. Her German publications include books on the needs of mathematically gifted children (1998), good tasks for the primary mathematics classroom (2003), and early childhood mathematics (2006). Currently she is a Professor of Mathematics Education at the University of Oldenburg, Germany.

Jana Slezáková was born in Nymburk, (formerly Czechoslovakia). Her schooling was in Prague. She obtained a masters degree as a secondary school teacher of mathematics and chemistry. Following this, she studied for a PhD in mathematics education, which she completed in 2000. During her doctoral studies she taught mathematics and chemistry at a technical college. Since 1998, she has taught mathematics education on the initial teacher education programme for primary teachers at the Faculty of Education, Charles University in Prague. Her research interests focus on early mathematical thinking.

Brigitte Spindeler was born in Borgholz, a small village in the middle of Germany. After training to teach at both primary and secondary level she taught in a primary school for several years. In 1998 she started her work at the University in Kassel and became involved in pre-service and in-service teacher training and research in the didactics of mathematics. As a lecturer she is currently working on a German adapted version of the Early Numeracy Research Project, which was developed at Monash University in Victoria, Australia, by Doug Clarke and his working group in 1999.

Fiona Thangata grew up in Norwich, England. After studying for a mathematics degree and qualifying as a teacher, she taught mathematics in secondary schools in England and Scotland. She then worked in in-service and pre-service education for primary and secondary mathematics teachers. Her doctoral research was on the use of ICT to enhance mathematical learning in the classroom. She has also taught in schools in the USA and Namibia. She is currently a Lecturer in Education at the University of East Anglia, Norwich, where she teaches on the initial teacher education programme (Primary PGCE).

Bernd Wollring was born in 1949 and raised in Westfalen, Germany. He qualified as a maths and physics teacher at the University of Münster before undertaking his doctoral studies in applied mathematics at the University of Heidelberg. Following research on young children's understanding of mathematics – with a particular focus on probability – he got docentship in mathematics education. He is currently a professor in mathematics education at the University of Kassel. His principal research interest is primary mathematics, specialising in geometry and assessment. He is active in international in-service teacher training and as an adviser working for the ministry of education of the state of Hessen.

Introduction

Mathematical Understanding 5–11 is about making mathematics more accessible: more accessible to teachers, student teachers, teacher educators, people generally interested in mathematics education and, most importantly, primary children. At the heart of this book and DVD lies the idea of communication: verbal, yes, but more significantly communication through action, creation, analysis and observation. The approach we adopt opens up avenues of mathematical learning to kinaesthetic, visual and verbal learners as well as to those who generally steer clear of mathematics and the anxieties sometimes associated with it.

Children's mathematical misconceptions frequently arise as a result of poor communication: everyone thinks they have understood but sometimes weeks – or even years – later, it is clear that this is not entirely the case. On numerous occasions we have seen understanding dawn when we teach topics such as subtraction, place value and shape to trainee primary teachers. We have observed, however, that people's understanding of mathematical concepts can be vastly improved if they have ample opportunities to demonstrate and discuss their thinking. This book provides such opportunities by presenting innovative ways of focusing on traditional mathematics curricula. It is primarily about broadening communication within the mathematics classroom and extending the ways in which fundamental principles and concepts might be presented in primary schools. It has been written for pre- and in-service teachers, teacher educators and anyone who has an interest in extending the ways children actively engage with mathematics. Teachers with English as an additional language (EAL) pupils in their class may find it of particular value as many of the activities discussed involve little or no verbal communication. We have also noted that children with special educational needs are attracted to many of the activities we have devised and demonstrate remarkable success with them.

This work originated from a three-year cross-cultural programme involving primary children, trainee and experienced teachers, teacher educators and researchers. It is based on a rigorous understanding of young children's mathematical development and all the activities discussed have been trialled – and refined – in a wide range of classrooms across Europe. I have been studying mathematics education in this country for many years[1] and what is exciting about this work is that it provides new dimensions to mathematics education which our research has clearly demonstrated are highly appealing to primary children *and* closely relate to current policy documents in England, Scotland, Wales and Northern Ireland. The wide spectrum of activities provide children with opportunities for discovery and creativity; scope to develop strategic approaches to their work and, perhaps most importantly, a sense of ownership and pride.

The tasks we present are not only innovative but are based around a series of themes firmly rooted in traditional primary mathematics curricula, making them entirely compatible with, for example, the revised National Numeracy Strategy (DfES, 2006). Thus, for instance, BlockCAD introduces children to the relationship between 3-D objects and their 2-D representations and enables them to develop their appreciation of key concepts through the medium of ICT.

As you will see noted in the biographical details, the authors of this book are all teacher educators but we come from very different traditions. Although we had different starting points, our intellectual journeys in mathematics education have led us all, however, to reach the following conclusions:

- Mathematics is a subject that the vast majority – in other words far more than are currently doing so – can enjoy.

- Understanding mathematical processes – rather than simply memorising facts – is the key to mathematical success.

- Most people are more than capable of grasping the fundamental principles of mathematics if they are presented in appropriate ways.

- Learners need to be provided with practical experiences and opportunities from which they can create their own understanding of a topic.

- Key to successful mathematics education is open and honest communication between teachers and pupils and between learners.

- It is important to cater for a range of learning styles so that children can acquire the necessary understanding and skills in ways best suited to their individual needs.

In the light of these shared beliefs, and following a conversation with Milan Hejný and Bernd Wollring, Andrea Peter-Koop brought us together in 2003 to bid for European funding under the Socrates Programme for transnational cooperation projects. Our COSIMA[2] application was successful and, for the past three years, we have been refining and trialling a range of activities which promote mathematical understanding, participation and enjoyment among primary children. We each began with learning environments with which we were familiar. Thus, for example, I selected subtraction as it plays a major role in the National Numeracy Strategy and yet I was aware that it is a topic potentially fraught with difficulties.

We have been very fortunate to work with groups of highly committed teachers in each of the project countries – Czech Republic, Germany and the UK as well as some from Slovakia. Some of these teachers were highly experienced having taught for over 30 years, others less so. Some had large and challenging classes of over 30 pupils while most had between 20 and 30 able, and not so able, children coming from a broad spectrum of urban and rural environments. Some of the schools were very well resourced with the latest equipment and the necessary expertise to operate it, while other teachers had very few resources and little experience of ICT. Whatever the circumstances, however, we found that the teachers and their pupils were all unfailingly cooperative; they were more than happy to trial and refine the ideas we presented to them and, crucially, they have since incorporated many of the project proposals into their everyday classroom practice. On the basis of this work our aims in writing this book and producing the accompanying DVD are:

- To introduce new practical ideas and approaches – based on the National Numeracy Strategy and international research – ready for use in the primary mathematics classroom.

- To develop teachers' and children's ability to use a range of communication strategies to enhance primary pupils' mathematical confidence and understanding.

- To provide innovative ways to assess children's developing understanding of mathematical thinking.

- To offer primary pre- and in-service teachers intriguing and thought-provoking professional development presented in an accessible manner.

We begin with a topic with which you will all be familiar – subtraction. On the face of it this is an easy topic but one which is susceptible to all manner of misconceptions. Often these do not surface until pupils are embarking on their secondary education and encountering algebra for the first time. By then the misconceptions are often deep rooted and surprisingly difficult to eradicate. In Chapter 1, therefore, I provide a slightly broader picture of subtraction than the one you might previously have encountered to enable you to more fully appreciate its subtleties and complexities. I also present a range of tried and tested strategies used successfully with young children, trainee and more experienced teachers across Europe. The ideas are not unduly taxing and, once understood, create a firm foundation on which learners can consolidate and develop their ability to use subtraction appropriately in both simple and relatively complex mathematical situations.

In Chapter 2 Brigitte Spindeler and Bernd Wollring focus on communicating ideas about shape and space. Again this is a topic with which young children are all too familiar: most of them spend much of their time rushing around or intricately involved in studying the minute detail – be it a spider or a spectrum – of the world around them. In so doing they use a range of skills including, in particular, their abilities to observe and analyse situations. Brigitte and Bernd capitalise on these skills in their chapter by linking children's interests and everyday mathematical ideas. For example, when pondering on how to make stars children develop an understanding of symmetry, proportion, paper folding and 2-D shapes. The activities Brigitte and Bernd discuss provide learners (including adults such as myself!) with many happy hours of challenging – and not so challenging – construction tasks. One of the beauties of this approach is that even some of the most reluctant mathematicians in a class will beaver away, use a variety of communication and learning styles and – although they will almost certainly be unaware of the fact – learn a considerable amount of mathematics in the process. I first became aware of this when one of the UK teachers in the study – David – reported that a couple of months after working on making stars, his class of eight-year-olds far exceeded his expectations when they undertook standard National Curriculum tasks (e.g. constructing polygons) on shape and space.

While Chapter 2 develops children's understanding of 3-D objects, Chapter 3 tackles the frequently misunderstood relationship between 2- and 3-D shapes. Over the many years I have spent as a teacher educator, I have often asked primary teachers how they introduce shape. The responses suggest a lot of uncertainty as to the best way to go about the topic. Indeed it is not uncommon for practitioners to introduce, for example, 2-D shapes followed by 3-D shapes one year, do the reverse the next and to present 2- and 3-D shapes simultaneously the year after. In their chapter – *Constructing and Connecting 2-* and *3-D shapes* – Diana Hunscheidt and Andrea Peter-Koop describe a computer generated program called BlockCAD. As will be apparent from the DVD, BlockCAD simulates the creation of models using the readily available children's construction toy Lego. Through the presentation of a variety of activities involving the use of Lego and the BlockCAD program – both together and separately – the relationships between 2- and 3-D shapes become more apparent. Indeed our work demonstrates that by using a combination of visual, kinaesthetic and, in some cases, oral communication children are far less likely to develop misunderstandings, with the added bonus that they actually enjoy the processes involved in their learning. As an important by-product, BlockCAD helps children develop a deeper understanding of IT. The program can be particularly beneficial for those lacking confidence in their technical abilities as it is both simple and fun to use.

Building on the use of ICT, Chapter 4 extends the notion of shape and space by introducing a further consideration – movement. Fiona Thangata and Alan Pagden describe in this chapter the concepts they consider relate well to national curricula on the development of functional thinking. The tried and tested activities they present are both popular with a wide age range of pupils (including the mathematically challenged) and provide an excellent foundation for work on angles and graphs which is often presented in the later primary years. Much of this detail is presented in the book but, to get more of a flavour of the possibilities available, I suggest that you combine your reading with watching the DVD.

In the past teachers have traditionally focused on pupils' mathematical knowledge rather than on the development of their mental abilities. Some less conventional tasks, however, highlight children's thinking processes with unexpected results. Thus, a teacher may be surprised, for example, by the high level of low achievers' creativity and resourcefulness when engaged in such activities. All chapters presented in this book are, to some extent, non-traditional and encourage the development of such abilities. Chapter 5 is fully devoted to this goal. The mathematical environment introduced in this chapter allows teachers to see how their pupils' abilities to, for example, classify, generalise, abstract, reason and make decisions are developed. Such an approach is excellent for cross-curricular work and allows pupils to transfer the mathematical content of a problem to other subjects such as language, science and literature.

In preparing this book we have been supported by many. In particular we are grateful to the European Socrates Programme for providing us with financial support.[3] We would also like to thank Helen Fairlie of Sage Publications for her faith in our abilities and her help and guidance in preparing and presenting our work. Other colleagues have provided invaluable support throughout the project. We will not mention them all by name – they know who they are – but we especially want to recognise the support of Ilka Ficken, Joey Schulze, Graham Littler, Birte Specht, Konrad Krainer and Gertraud Benke. Finally, we are most indebted to all the children, trainee and experienced teachers in the Czech Republic, Germany, Slovakia and the UK who gave so generously of their time and whose feedback proved to be so thought-provoking and constructive. It is to them that we dedicate this book.

Anne D. Cockburn

Endnotes

[1]   See, for example, Desforges and Cockburn, 1987; Cockburn, 1999; Haylock and Cockburn, 1997, 2003.

[2]   COSIMA is an abbreviation of communicating our strategies in primary school mathematics.

[3]   Grant number 112091-CP-1-Comenius-C21.

References

Cockburn, A.D. (1999) *Teaching Mathematics with Insight*. London: Falmer Press.

Department for Education and Skills (DfES) (2006) *Primary Framework for Literacy and Mathematics*. London: DfES.

Desforges, C. and Cockburn, A.D. (1987) *Understanding the Mathematics Teacher: A Study of First School Practice*. Lewes: Falmer Press.

Haylock, D.W. and Cockburn, A.D. (1997) *Understanding Mathematics in the Lower Primary Years (2nd edition)*. London: Paul Chapman Publishing.

Haylock, D.W. and Cockburn, A.D. (2003) *Understanding Mathematics in the Lower Primary Years: A Guide for Teachers of Children 3–8*. London: Paul Chapman Publishing.

References to Mathematical concepts covered in *Mathematical Understanding 5-11*

*taken from *Primary National Strategy* Primary Framework for Mathematics (2006), p88–101. Key objectives and Early Learning Goals (ELGs) in the Foundation Stage are highlighted in **bold type**. The publication is available for download from: www.standards.dfes.gov.uk/primaryframeworks

Mathematical topics	Chapter 1	Chapter 2	Chapter 3	Chapter 4	Chapter 5	English Framework Primary Framework for Mathematics key objectives*
USING AND APPLYING MATHEMATICS	✓	✓	✓	✓	✓	Foundation Stage (p88) **Use developing mathematical ideas and methods to solve practical problems** **Talk about recognise and recreate simple patterns** (N.B. there are no key objectives for Y1–Y6 (p88–89) However, progression in communication, reasoning, enquiry and problem-solving are embedded within this strand).
CALCULATING Subtraction:	✓					Foundation Stage (p94) **In practical activities and discussion begin to use the vocabulary involved in...subtracting.**
	✓					Year 1 (p94) **Use the vocabulary related to ...subtraction and symbols to describe and record...subtraction number sentences.**
Subtraction: Partitioning (taking away)	✓					Foundation Stage (p94) **Begin to relate... subtraction to 'taking away'**
Partitioning (taking away)	✓					Year 1 (p94) Understand subtraction as 'take away'...by counting up
Comparison (difference between)	✓					Year 1 (p94) Understand subtraction as...find a 'difference' by counting up
Inverse of addition structure	✓					Year 2 (p94) Understand that subtraction is the inverse of addition
Complement of a set structure	✓					*Implicit in* *Year 2 (p94)* *Use the symbols...-....and = to record and interpret number sentences involving all four operations; calculate the value of an unknown in a number sentence (e.g. 30 -[]= 24)*

Mathematical topics	Chapter 1	Chapter 2	Chapter 3	Chapter 4	Chapter 5	English Framework Primary Framework for Mathematics key objectives*
UNDERSTANDING SHAPE (GEOMETRY)		✓				Foundation Stage (p96) **Use language such as 'circle' or 'bigger' to describe the shape and size of solids and flat shapes.**
		✓	✓	✓		Use everyday words to describe position
		✓	✓			Year 1 (p96) **Visualise and name common 2-D shapes and 3-D solids and describe their features; use them to make patterns, pictures and models**
		✓	✓			Year 2 (p96) **Visualise common 2-D shapes and 3-D solids; identify shapes from pictures of them in different positions and orientations; sort, make and describe shapes, referring to their properties.**
			✓	✓		Year 2 (p96) Follow and give instructions involving position, direction and movement
			✓	✓		Year 2 (p96) Recognise and use whole, half and quarter turns… Identify reflective symmetry.
				✓		Year 4 (p97) **Know that angles are measured in degrees and that one whole turn is 360°; compare and order angles less than 180°**
		✓		✓		Year 5 (p97) **…recognise parallel and perpendicular lines in grids and shapes**
MEASURING						Year 6 (p99) **Solve problems by measuring, estimating and calculating**
					✓	Foundation Stage(p88) **Talk about, recognise and recreate simple patterns**

HANDLING DATA

Objective			
Year 1 (p100) Use diagrams to sort objects into groups according to a given criterion, suggest a different criterion for grouping the same objects.	/		
Year 2 (p100) **Use…diagrams to sort objects; explain choices using appropriate language, including 'not'**	/		
Year 3 (p100) Use… Carroll diagrams to sort data and objects using more than one criterion.	/		
Year 4 (p101) **Answer a question by identifying what data to collect; organise, present, analyse and interpret the data in tables, diagrams, tally charts, pictograms and bar charts, using ICT where appropriate.**	/	/	
Year 6 (p101) **Solve problems by collecting, selecting, processing, presenting and interpreting data, using ICT where appropriate; draw conclusions and identify further questions to ask.**	/	/	/

CHAPTER 1

Understanding Subtraction through Enhanced Communication

Anne D. Cockburn

Communicating the Theme

Sam – a young and enthusiastic trainee teacher – asked the class, 'What is the difference between 7 and 6?'. Jo's hand shot up and he immediately responded, 'Well seven is all straight lines and sixes are all curly'.

Teaching subtraction is harder than teaching addition for several reasons. One – as graphically illustrated by Jo's response – is the use of words which have different meanings in different contexts: 'difference', 'take away', 'the same as', to name but a few. Another reason why subtraction can be difficult to teach is that people have a tendency to make some kinds of comparisons and not others. For example, a child will quite happily say, 'I am taller than my brother' or 'I have more pencils than Sandy'. But, how often have your heard comments such as, 'It's not fair, I've got 8 less than him!', or 'It's wonderful those cakes cost much more than those ones'. In this chapter I will explain more about subtraction and explore why some children find it hard to understand. I will then provide a selection of activities which encourage a range of different communication strategies which have been used successfully with children and adults both in the UK and the other COSIMA countries.

Communicating the Concepts

We all use subtraction frequently. Most of us probably use it everyday...

- when you buy five cream cakes, eat one and wonder whether you will have enough of them left for your visitors;
- when you compare your results on a test with a colleague;
- when you work out whether you have enough money to buy something.

My observations suggest, however, that surprisingly few people understand the range of basic concepts involved. If you had to describe subtraction what would you say? Would it be along the lines of 'taking away' or 'finding the difference between two values'? Would you add anything else or do you think that covers it? When I asked 168 primary teacher training students at the beginning of their mathematics course, 75% defined subtraction as 'taking away', 8% said that it was 'the difference between two numbers' with a further 9% considering it to be both. Of the remaining 8%, only one gave a slightly more complete explanation saying that, 'Subtraction can mean various things such as "take away" or "less than"'.

In the past, subtraction was typically taught as 'taking away': it was easy to demonstrate and children could quickly relate it to their own experiences of 'taking away' – or eating – biscuits; 'taking away' – or losing – toys and so on. More formally this type of subtraction is called *partitioning*: you start with a certain number of items, some are removed in some way (e.g. eaten, spent, stolen) and the question is, 'How many are left?'. This is illustrated by the cream cake example above and in Figure 1.1a. The partitioning method of subtraction is introduced to four- and five-year-old children in the UK in the first year of formal schooling.

Typically pictorial representations of partitioning involve two groups of items distinctly separated as in Figure 1.1a but it is important to provide children with a range of illustrations – such as in Figures 1.1b and 1.1c – to demonstrate that the same principle applies whatever the arrangement of the items presented. Ideally teachers can demonstrate the processes involved in subtraction by physically undertaking a variety of activities such as eating a cherry from a bag of ten; breaking a biscuit from a newly opened packet and asking how many whole ones are left and so on.

Recently UK teachers have been encouraged to teach five- and six-year-olds 'difference between' – also known as the *comparison structure*. This is the structure you would use when comparing marks in a test as described above. Children typically use this structure when comparing their ages or who has more biscuits (see Figure 1.2a). Questions relating to this structure are generally of the type:

- 'What is the difference between... ?'
- 'How many more in... ?'
- 'How many fewer in... ?'

Interestingly, children tend to use 'more' rather than 'fewer' in their conversations but it is important that teachers give them experience of both, emphasising, for example, that in Figure 1.2a Sam has three fewer biscuits than Jo, as represented by $5 - 2 = 3$, and Jo has three more sweets than Sam, also represented by $5 - 2 = 3$.

Again, I would suggest that learners are provided with a range of representations and examples so that they develop a deeper understanding of the comparison structure. The examples given in Figure 1.2b are good starting points for a discussion. With older children comparisons can also be made in a range of settings where pictures provide less tangible support: such as comparing the speeds of cars or the volumes of irregular objects.

Figure 1.1a *An example of the partitioning method of subtraction*

Figure 1.1b *An alternative example of partitioning*

Figure 1.1c *Another example of partitioning*

Figure 1.2a   *An example of the comparison model of subtraction*

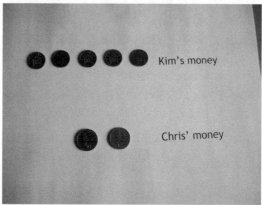

Figure 1.2b   *Other examples of the comparison model of subtraction*

In Year 2 (six- and seven-year-olds) UK children are often introduced to a third type of subtraction: *the inverse of addition structure*. This is illustrated by the earlier example when you wanted to know whether you had sufficient money to buy something. This is usually rather more difficult than the partitioning and comparison structures for children as it typically involves questions such as, 'How much more do I need?' or 'What must be added to 3 pence to make 10 pence?'. As discussed further below, in such cases children frequently latch onto words such as 'more' and 'added' and therefore they frequently add rather than subtract. A further danger looms if you wish to use a practical demonstration. For example, if you produce both 3 pence and 10 pence (as you might if it were a comparison), you might be given the answer 13 pence when what you really wanted to know was: if you had 3 pence how much more money would you need to buy a sweet costing 10 pence.

There are two other structures primary children need to become familiar with if they are to have a good grounding in subtraction before they proceed to more advanced mathematics. The first is the *complement of a set – or union – structure* which may, at first sight, appear rather awkward but which, in reality, is used quite frequently in everyday life. Here the word 'not' – or something similar – is typically used. For example:

- I have made 8 sandwiches, 5 already have butter on them, how many do not?
- There are 25 children on the class register but only 22 children came in today, how many are not here?

The other type of subtraction involves the *reduction structure* and this is probably most commonly encountered during the sales when items are reduced: a coat costs £100 in December but is reduced to £75 in the January sales. In many ways the reduction structure is similar to that of partitioning but there is one notable difference. When taking away – or partitioning – you are working with problems which may be represented with real objects but, when reducing, this need not necessarily be the case. For example, yesterday the temperature was 6°C but overnight it dropped by 10°C; what is the temperature now? A number line can be a good way to illustrate such problems, as shown in Figure 1.3. As will be discussed further below, although they are similar, experience with both reduction and partitioning structures is crucial if children are to have a sound understanding on which to build when they encounter more advanced mathematics and, in particular, algebra.

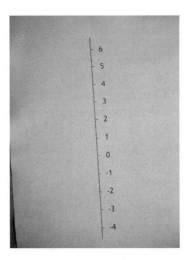

Figure 1.3   *Example of how a number line might be used when working with the reduction structure*

Prior to recent reviews of primary mathematics teaching in the UK, teachers tended to focus on the products of children's work making it difficult to assess their understanding. Indeed, in my work with Charles Desforges in the 1980s, we discovered that in almost one in four cases, children were not solving calculations in the way their teachers had anticipated: some were getting the correct answers without doing any mathematics whatsoever! For example, some individuals copied someone else's work while others looked back at earlier examples of their own work that had already been marked by the teacher. More often that not, children's ploys went undetected by their teachers. Also, as discussed above, sometimes children's responses were constructed using different information to that predicted by the teacher. For example, Mrs T asked her class of five-year-olds, 'If there were 5 apples in the fruit bowl and you ate 2 of them, how many would be left?'. Mia replied '4'. When Mrs T asked Mia to explain she said, 'I'm never allowed to take 2 apples so I only ate one and so there were 4 left'.

Now, UK teachers are expected to invite their pupils to explain how they arrive at their solutions, encouraging the children to focus on their thinking processes and understanding. Some do this well; others less so. Sometimes the latter teachers lack confidence in their own mathematical abilities. Sometimes they prefer to continue using the more traditional methods in which they were trained. Sometimes they think they are providing opportunities for children to share their ideas and explain their different strategies when, in fact, they may be encouraging pupils to use – and discuss – a specific method. Take, for example, the case of Mrs R[1] and her class of five-year-olds.

Mrs R: Who can tell me the answer to 20 subtract 11?

Jude: 9

Mrs R: Good! Now tell us how you did it?

Jude: Well I counted back from 20 to 11 and got to 9.

Mrs R: Mmm. Did anybody do it any other way?

Sally: Well I put 11 in my head and counted up to 20 using my fingers and I ended up with 9 fingers.

Mrs R: Mmm. Any other suggestions on how you might subtract 11 from 20? Remember what we did yesterday.

Molly: Well I know that 20 minus 10 is 10 and 11 is one more than 10 so the answer must be 9.

Mrs R: Great. Well done Molly. Now everyone, remember those number facts you learnt last night when you are doing your maths today.

Mrs R's actions were understandable if her principle aim was to teach her class an efficient way to subtract using known number facts; however, in guiding her class towards her preferred method she may be discouraging them from thinking through – and retaining – potentially successful strategies for themselves. Thinking about how you learnt to use a computer may illustrate the point more vividly. Taking my own case, my most effective learning has been when I have had to struggle through trial and error rather than through having a computer genius show me which buttons to press. Returning to the classroom, Mrs R's technique may not work so well if you have a poor memory coupled with a lack of understanding of subtraction. If, however, children are exposed to a range of strategies – including their own – they can begin to develop a greater appreciation of how numbers can be manipulated and more of an understanding of how they might tackle subtraction problems in a manner which suits their current knowledge and expertise. (As an aside, the learning of times-tables seems to go in and out of fashion: it is fine if you know that 90mm x 70mm is 6300mm when you are making a rectangular cake but what can you do if you cannot remember that 9 x 7 = 63 and you have no calculator to hand? Having the facility to both estimate and work from first principles means that you are likely to be much more successful when you attempt to work out whether the size of the cake you ordered is better suited to an individual or a large party.)

One of the underlying principles of this book is that children develop authentic mathematical understanding if they construct meaning from their own mathematical efforts while, at the same time, observing and reflecting on others' ideas and strategies. Thus, it may be that they do not tackle subtraction problems in the most efficient way to start with. Rather they complete their work in a way that has meaning for them and through a range of processes – discussions with teachers, other children, games, everyday life, observations and so on – they construct and refine the processes they use until they are both effective (i.e. they get the calculations correct through the application of their understanding) and efficient (i.e. they can solve problems quickly). Without such an evolution in their mathematical thinking we would argue that the chances of children making errors are much higher and they may well have inadequate foundations on which to build.

To summarise: there are several different subtraction structures and, in order to develop a sound understanding of the concepts involved, it is important to use and discuss a variety of them.

In the remainder of this chapter I will provide a range of strategies that we have invited students and teachers to use both in UK and elsewhere. The focus in all cases is to introduce primary children and both future and experienced teachers to a wealth of mathematical opportunities in a child-centred manner.

Communicating Experiences with Pre-service Teachers

As discussed above, few trainee teachers have a sound understanding of subtraction. Obviously the various structures can be described to them but, as with children, to gain a real appreciation of subtraction, they need to be exposed to a range of experiences and construct their own knowledge and understanding of the concepts involved. In this section I will present some tried and tested strategies we have used with student teachers both in the UK and elsewhere.

Being able to visualise situations can prove very helpful when trying to decide how to respond to a given problem. For example, reflect on what goes on in your mind when I say, 'I had 6 eggs, I used 2 to make a cake, how many did I have left for breakfast?'. As a warm-up activity you might ask students to match the pictures and problems given in Figure 1.4 and discuss their responses with a partner. Assuming that this activity presents few – if any – difficulties, you could ask the students to match the problems given in Figure 1.5 to the calculations presented. You could then encourage them to sketch pictures of the problems. Such a task very much mirrors what students might be required to do with young children and it also provides a good indication of their understanding. Discussion with a student partner should be encouraged as it presents an ideal opportunity to talk mathematically and articulate thinking. Hopefully, through conversation, the students will begin to understand that, although pictures can prove extremely useful, it is not always easy to represent mathematical problems pictorially in an accurate and helpful way. For example the following is misleading:

6	take away	2	equals ?
* * * * * *		* *	

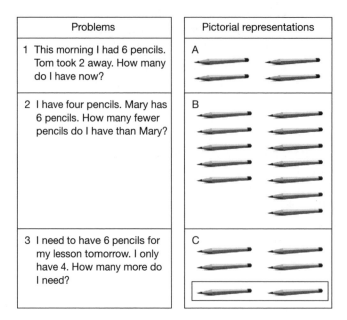

Figure 1.4   Sample of matching tasks for trainee teachers

Problem	Calculation
1 John has 8 cars. 3 are large. If all the others are small, how many are small?	A ? + 3 = 8
2 Simon has 8 pencils. He loses 3. How many does he have left?	B 8 = 3 + ?
3 Bianca has some marbles. She bought 3 more. Now she has 8. How many did she have to start with?	C 8 – 3 = ?

Figure 1.5   A sample of problems and the corresponding calculations to match

As I will discuss further below, I am against young children formally committing their mathematics to paper before they have a very solid grounding in the concepts involved. This notwithstanding, it is important that future primary teachers can convert mathematical problems into equations and vice versa. Thus, for example, we divide trainees into two groups. The first are given the problems shown in Figure 1.6 and the second the number sentences. The tasks are either to produce appropriate equations or create suitable problems to match the problems and then compare and contrast the results. Such exercises can prove to be useful catalysts for discussion about the equals sign (=) and the difficulties some children encounter when faced with examples such as 10 = 6 + ? (see also below). It is also worth noting that discrete (i.e. involving countable objects) and continuous (e.g. ages and weights) examples are used in Figure 1.6. It is important that trainee teachers and their future pupils become familiar with both. In passing, if you were using a calculator, all of the problems would be solved by visualising them as 10 – 6 = ?

Problem	Number sentences	=
1 Sarah wants 10 cars. She already has 6. How many more does she need?	$6 + ? = 10$	
2 (a) Jenny is 10 years old. David is 6. What is the difference in their ages? (b) Fred has a statue which weighed 10 kilograms. The head dropped off. It weighed 6 kilograms. How much does the statue weigh now?	$10 - 6 = ?$	
3 At 9am Bryony had a bucket of water. She added 6 litres. Now there are 10 litres in the bucket. How much water did she have in the bucket at 9am?	$? + 6 = 10$	
4 Miss Brown would like 10 of her students to understand subtraction. She knows that 6 of them already have a good understanding. How many will she need to teach?	$10 = 6 + ?$	

Figure 1.6   *Example discussion exercise in creating equations and problems*

As part of their training it is also important that student teachers become familiar with resources commonly used in primary mathematics classrooms. These tend to go in and out of fashion and include equipment such as number lines, multilink and cuisinaire rods. Trainees' familiarity with these resources may depend on their age and where they attended primary school. For example, until relatively recently the number line was frequently used in mainland Europe but was rarely used in UK primary classrooms. Extending the activities associated with Figure 1.6 to include consideration of appropriate resources is a very informative exercise and, again, can reveal who has a good understanding of subtraction problems and the ways in which they might best be represented. The DVD (Item 1.1) includes examples of how student teachers in Germany used Duplo to illustrate various subtraction structures involving 8, 5 and 3.

A key part of a student teacher's preparation is their time spent in school. We very much encourage our students to observe experienced teachers in action, note their techniques and discuss the thinking behind sessions. Unfortunately, as illustrated above with Mrs R, teachers do not always operate in a way we would recommend and thus it is important that students discuss their observations on their return to college and consider why teachers sometimes behave in unexpected ways.

Working in schools provides an excellent opportunity for students to see young children engaged in mathematical activities. For many years we have asked trainees to note down any mathematical errors pupils make. A sample of these is presented in Figure 1.7a. As part of the task the students are encouraged to talk to their pupils and pose questions which will elicit the children's thought processes. This exercise seems to be another effective way to assess trainees' understanding but it also encourages them to think beyond the children's responses and begin to consider how a learner might be thinking and why they might be thinking like that. This, in turn, helps trainees to reflect on their own practice and the opportunities they might provide for their pupils to reduce the likelihood of errors. Thus, if a child who wrote $101 - 9 = 2$ had had more experience of associating quantities of items to their numerical representation, they might have realised that their response of 2 was inappropriate. The error was almost certainly due to an insufficient understanding of place value rather than subtraction but, as is often the case, misconceptions may come to light unexpectedly. As an aside, all too rarely in my view do children see – let alone touch – more than about 20 objects in a classroom activity so it is not entirely surprising that they have little understanding of place value and the quantities large numbers represent.

Task	Child's response
Zubin had 7 sweets. Jack had 10. How many more sweets did Jack have than Zubin?	7 + 10 = 17
Sally scored 6 goals and Natasha scored 14. What was the difference between the scores?	6 – 14 = 0
52 – 47 =	52 – 47 = 15
101 – 9 =	101 – 9 = 2
3 – 2 = *** **	5
Using a number line calculate: 8 – 5 =	4

Figure 1.7a   Examples of children's mathematical errors

Having considered Figure 1.7a, how would you explain the errors? Take a minute to reflect on your responses and then you might like to compare them with those of the students as presented in Figure 1.7b.

Child's response	Student teachers' explanation
7 + 10 = 17	Zoe had difficulty reading the problem but she recognised the word 'more' and so she added 7 and 10.
6 – 14 = 0	Ben wrote down the numbers in the order they were given and explained that the answer must be 0 as he had been presented with an impossible situation.
52 – 47 = 15	Mia has an insufficient understanding of place value and, for example, thinks of 52 as 5 and 2. The problem is compounded by the fact that she believes that you always take the smaller number from the larger. Hence she did 5 – 4 and then 7 – 2.
101 – 9 = 2	John does not appreciate that 0 acts as a place holder and has a significant part to play, thus 101 is not 11.
5	The stars underneath the figures were intended to remind Sam of the values associated with 3 and 2. Sam was delighted when she explained that there was no need to look at the numbers as all she had to do was count the stars.
4	I observed Kai using the number line but incorrectly, i.e. he started at 8 and counted all the numbers back to, and including, 4.

Figure 1.7b   Student teachers' explanation for the errors shown in Figure 1.7a

To summarise: successful trainee teachers need to acquire a sound understanding of subtraction and all its many guises. They need to become comfortable discussing – with colleagues and children – the teaching and learning issues surrounding it and be adept at demonstrating a range of ways to illustrate the various subtraction structures.

Communicating Activities for the Classroom

As mentioned above, young children have experience of subtraction in their everyday lives. As a teacher it is important that you capitalise on these experiences so that your pupils can build on their developing understanding of the concept. There are several ways to do this, many of which will be familiar to experienced teachers. For example you might invite the parents in for an evening of primary mathematics. Recently a local school did this and they were overwhelmed by the numbers who attended and their responses. Their success was in part due to excellent publicity and in part to the exciting activities the parents were invited to try. I suspect quite a few were surprised by how much they learnt and how little they had previously understood! Joint home/school projects can also prove very successful, although care needs to be taken that parents do not engage in too much 'teaching' as this can result in what Constance Kamii has described as 'mindless techniques that serve only as tricks' (1985: 103). Activities which can encourage home/school teamwork might include baking, model making and games (see below) all of which can include elements of subtraction and opportunities for much discussion. Talking to a colleague – Ralph – over coffee, he immediately volunteered that playing darts was an excellent way to learn subtraction: motivation is high and the pressures sometimes associated with the mathematics classroom are low. Having a number line and a 100-square close by can prove handy aids initially although these may raise some eyebrows if your darts playing is in a pub!

Everyday activities in school are a useful way to demonstrate the relevance of subtraction in real life situations. This need not be either time consuming or a major event – although it can be should you wish – but rather it is an opportunity for the children to see you use mathematics and to observe you adopting a range of strategies to solve problems. As a brief aside: from time to time I ask primary pupils why we need to learn about numbers and whether they have ever seen adults use them. A response which still sticks out in my mind – albeit more than 20 years after it was given – came from Ben who explained that his Mum had last used numbers '... about nine months ago ... no ... a year ago, when we moved house, Mummy had to count pegs to put the curtains up with' (Desforges and Cockburn, 1987: 100). Amusing perhaps but also somewhat disturbing as this is one of the few responses I have ever encountered where a child has been able to describe seeing an adult using numbers. To return to the classroom: you could ask your pupils why they use numbers and, indeed, whether they have observed adults doing so. You might ask them – as Jackie did – for their definitions of subtraction. Interestingly her class of seven- and eight-year-olds gave more impressive answers than the student teachers mentioned above! More specifically the children described subtraction as:

Taking away

Opposite to adding

You take a number from a higher number

It's counting back

Dividing is repetition subtraction

Minus

Find the difference

You might find it revealing to ask the class to write number stories to match each of the above words and phrases.

There are everyday opportunities to use subtraction when taking the register (e.g. you can practise partitioning when you ask: 'There are 25 names on the register. 5 children are absent. How many children are here today?'[2]); when handing out resources (e.g. you could focus on the complement of a set structure when you pose the following question: 'I have 12 crayons. I am going to give 6 of them to Bob. How many will be left for me?'[3]) and when setting up teams (e.g. the comparison structure may be illustrated by: 'There are 5 children in group A but only 3 in group B. How many more do I need in group B to make 5?') and so on. Sometimes you might want to model the technique you use to solve the problem – for example by drawing a quick number line and counting back the number of children who are absent. Sometimes you might decide to invite the children to explain their strategies for reaching a solution and sometimes you might not say anything at all because time is short which, in effect, allows you to model another way in which calculations may be done, that is quickly and quietly in one's head. Songs and poems are another mathematically low stress way to practise subtraction. Sometimes to add a bit of variety and fun you, as the teacher, can make a deliberate mistake. Our observations suggest that children very much enjoy this and are only too willing to explain in detail what you have done wrong and why. Although I suggest usually doing these activities in a low key way I would advise that, from time to time, you remind the children that they are doing subtraction. Jackie, for example, discovered that her class were amazed to learn that they had actually been subtracting successfully when some of them found 'mathematics' something difficult and to be avoided.

More formal opportunities for communicating subtraction strategies can occur in oral mental starters at the beginning of mathematics sessions. Here it is a question of sharing ideas and strategies rather than a teacher imposing his or her view of subtraction and how it might be done. The following extract shows David working with a class of eight-year-olds on a range of subtraction structures at the start of a mathematics session.

T: Now the questions are not difficult. What I am interested in is how you explain what you have done. Here we go. 'Peter has 26 pieces of fruit. 9 are apples. How many pieces are there of other types of fruit?'. [Children write their responses on individual boards and hold them up for the teacher to see.] Okay we've all got the same answer. Tim, what calculation did you actually do?

Tim: I minused 10 and added on one.

T: So you minused 10 from 26 and added on one. Did anybody do it a different way? Sam?

Sam: Well I know that 6 is just 3 less than 9 and take away 3 from 20.

T: Explain that again for me.

Sam: 6 is 3 less than 9.

T: Why is that important to you then? Why is it important that 6 is 3 less than 9?

Sam: 'Cos if I take away 3 from 20 …

T: From 26? So you counted back 6 then you counted back another 3?

Sam: Yes.

T: Here is the second one: 'I made 35 cakes and I ate 7 of them, how many are left?'. Caitlin how did you do it?

Caitlin: I know that 7 was 2 more than 5 so I took 5 from 35 and I took 2 more off.

T: Okay so we split the 7 into a 5 to count back and then another 2 to get 28. Any other ways?

Jo: Take off 10 and add on 3.

T: Okay, take off 10 and then add on 3. Next question: 'Wendy wants 50 stamps. She has 17. How many more does she need?' How was that question different to the first two?

Pat: I did it as an add.

T: You did it as an add? So what made you add that question where you may have subtracted on the first two? What was it that was crucial about that question which meant that adding was easier than subtraction? What made you add rather than subtract?

Pat: I know that 17 add 3 was 20, and 20 add 30 was 50.

T: So you counted up in two steps almost like imagining a number line. Counting on 3 and then counting on however many tens you need to jump on. Did anyone do it as a subtraction? Did anyone actually take the number away from 50? Arthur how did you take 17 from 50.

Arthur: I took 17 away from 50 by just knowing it, by just doing it, by taking 50 minus 40 and then minus the 7.

T: So you did 50 take away 10 to leave you with 40 and then you took away 7. Another slightly different way?

Alex: Take away 20 and add on 3.

T: Take away 20 and add on 3.

Games can be a good way to encourage children to think about subtraction and to share their methods of calculation with each other. For example *I have, who has?* is a game which can be adapted to suit a range of group sizes and abilities. A miniature version is presented in Figure 1.8. In essence you have the same number of players as you have cards. Thus there would be three players for Figure 1.8 – which would be a very small number for a typical game. Each player has a card and player A begins the game by saying, 'Who has the difference between 5 and 3?'. Player B might then respond, 'I have 2. Who has 8 minus 5?' and then player C might say, 'I have 3. Who has 10 subtract 6?' and so on. Following each response there is an opportunity for the teacher – or indeed another child – to say, 'I disagree. How did you calculate that?'. Using such a strategy every time allows pupils to check each other's answers and demonstrate their thinking. An example of this game[4] is shown on the DVD (Items 1.2a and 1.2b).

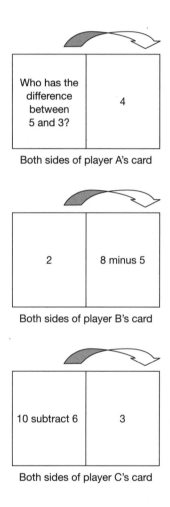

Both sides of player A's card

Both sides of player B's card

Both sides of player C's card

Figure 1.8   *A miniature version of* I have, who has?

A similar idea is to make use of a bingo game. Working with a partner, each pair of children is given a card with a range of numbers on it as illustrated in Figure 1.9a. (The numbers on each of the cards differ and, for example, you may wish to arrange it so that the more confident children have higher numbers which correspond to the more challenging questions.) The 'caller' – usually the teacher in the first instance – has a set of questions, a possible sample of which is given in Figure 1.9b. The caller asks a question which each pair consider and discuss. If the answer to the question features on their card then they may cover it up. The first children to cover all the numbers on their card are the winners. The accompanying DVD (Items 1.3a, 1.3b and 1.3c) shows a small group playing bingo.

4	10	5	9	8
7	3	4	0	2
1	0	5	10	6

Figure 1.9a   A sample bingo card

> 4 subtract 2?
> What is the difference between 0 and 10?
> If I started with 6 cakes and ate 2 of them, how many would be left?
> 7 minus 3?

Figure 1.9b   Sample bingo questions

Working in a classroom recently, I saw two very delighted children when they made the discovery that subtracting the following pairs of numbers always produced an answer of 10: 41 subtract 31; 29 subtract 19; 95 subtract 85. The revelation came about when they were set some questions and invited to use a 100 square, such as shown in Figure 1.10, to help them. It was a real pleasure to see how a relatively simple exercise could give two low attaining children insight into both subtraction strategies and place value.

1	2	3	4	5	6	7	8	9	10
11	12	13	14	15	16	17	18	19	20
21	22	23	24	25	26	27	28	29	30
31	32	33	34	35	36	37	38	39	40
41	42	43	44	45	46	47	48	49	50
51	52	53	54	55	56	57	58	59	60
61	62	63	64	65	66	67	68	69	70
71	72	73	74	75	76	77	78	79	80
81	82	83	84	85	86	87	88	89	90
91	92	93	94	95	96	97	98	99	100

Figure 1.10   A 100 square

Unfortunately some teachers are not so lucky in their choice of resources. For example some people argue that money is a useful way to teach subtraction. They set up shops to encourage young children to buy and sell things and introduce the idea of giving change as a means of practising subtraction. While the idea is perhaps reasonable from an adult perspective, some children can quickly become confused. To a certain extent this is because they usually see their parents using credit cards to purchase items in shops rather than cash. More pertinently here, however, is the fact that some children are introduced to subtraction before they have a sound concept of numbers and what they represent. For example the children who tend to enjoy role play – such as four- and five-year-olds – may view a 10 pence coin as worth '1' rather than representing 10 pence. Similarly they might see a £1 coin as worth '1'. Thus if they paid for an item costing 10 pence with a £1 coin they would not predict the need for any change to be included as part of the transaction. Obviously with older pupils who have a firmer concept of number this is unlikely to be a major issue, although for these pupils, the time for playing shops has usually long gone.

As children develop in their understanding the mathematical tasks they face are likely to become more abstract but it is important that you as their teacher are able to refer them to practical illustrations. Many, for example, are perplexed when they first encounter equations such as 3 + ? = 7 or, even more troubling for those who do not have a sound grasp of the meaning of the equals sign, 6 = ? + 2. If you can 'translate' these into real life problems and encourage your pupils to do so as well, then understanding will be much enhanced.

Similarly it is important for children to realise that familiar resources can be adapted to help them solve more complex problems. As shown in Figure 1.11, for example, Audrey's class found the empty number line very useful when first confronted with the following problem: 'One stick took 3 minutes 15 seconds to travel under the bridge. Another took 2 minutes 20 seconds. What's the difference?'.

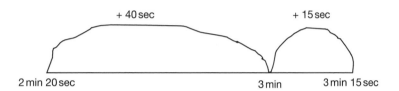

Figure 1.11   Example of how a specifically tailored number line may be used to solve a problem

To summarise, as teachers we need to be very aware that our pupils may have a range of very different perspectives to our own. If they are to develop a sound understanding of the basic subtraction concepts, it is important to ensure that discussion and practical demonstrations play a key role in mathematics sessions. Children's ideas should be shared and celebrated both with you and their peers.

Communicating Ideas for In-service Courses

Earlier in the chapter I pointed out that some children can explain subtraction more fully than trainee primary teachers; a good starting point for in-service teachers, therefore, might be to ask them to write down what they understand by the term 'subtraction'. Their responses are likely to give you an indication of how best to proceed. It may well be that you will have quite a broad range of knowledge and understanding in a teachers' group in which case working in mixed ability groups and encouraging dialogue could prove to be one of several effective strategies you use. Thus you might ask teachers to work in small groups of three or four and complete the matching tasks presented in Figures 1.4 and 1.5 for students.

Another approach which works well is to invite teachers to trial tasks intended for children. For example, they could consider how they might use the empty number line to demonstrate finding the difference between large numbers and then you might produce some children's work – such as that from Russell's class in Figure 1.12 – for discussion. Such an approach can shield the less confident from revealing their relative lack of understanding and it can also be used as an illustration of how pupils' ideas may differ but all be equally valid.

Find the difference between 582 and 47

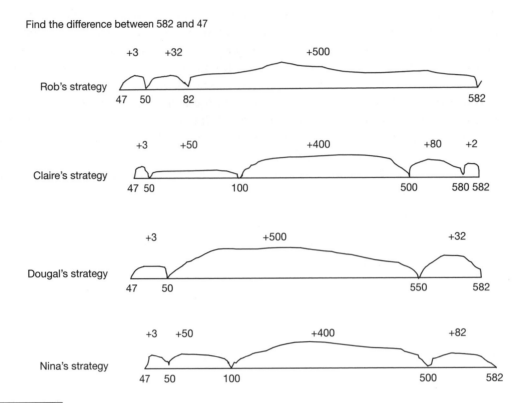

Figure 1.12   *Children's strategies for calculating differences using the number line*

Some of the members of an in-service group may have trained well before practitioners were encouraged to focus on processes rather than products. Introducing them to trainee teachers' thinking on children's errors – as discussed with reference to Figures 1.7a and 1.7b above – has proved to be an excellent way to encourage such individuals to think about mathematics from different perspectives. These thoughts can then be extended by inviting them to think of two or more strategies for working with a child who has one of the misconceptions described above.

Reviewing tasks used by teachers in other countries also appears to be a non-threatening way to approach topics such as subtraction which, in a broad sense may be unfamiliar to some experienced teachers. By way of example Milan – working with children in the Czech Republic – gave a group eight strips of paper (see Figure 1.13) and asked them to sort them into two stories each made up of four pieces of paper. The strips were not numbered and were mixed up, unlike those in Figure 1.13.

> 1 On the top shelf there are 9 books.
> 2 On the bottom shelf there are 2 books.
> 3 What is the difference between the 2 shelves?
> 4 There are 7 books.
> 5 On the shelf there are 8 books.
> 6 I took away 3 books.
> 7 How many books are there on the shelf?
> 8 There are 5 books.

Figure 1.13   *Phrases used in a Czech number story task*

If it does not arise spontaneously, it is worthwhile posing the question, 'What might you do if a child started their story with statement (1) followed by (6) and then announced that they were stuck?'

An important aspect of any in-service course on subtraction is that teachers come away from it with a clear appreciation as to why primary children need to develop a broad understanding of the topic. For most it will mean that you need to provide them with a Eureka – or 'Ah' – type experience for, as I have implied, many will have come on your course without such insight. My eyes were opened when I started thinking about differences in summer and winter temperatures and had to think in terms of positive and negative numbers. It happened in a flash and I am embarrassed to think, not only how old I was at the time, but also how many mathematics exams I had successfully passed on the way to this revelation! I wonder how much else I did not fully comprehend and whether this hampered my progress...

My advice is to provide simple – but powerful – illustrations which enable teachers to discover for themselves why their understanding may be incomplete. One of the reasons that, in my view, they need to be shocked into a new understanding is that both research and personal experience have shown me that old habits die very hard. I had always been used to simply taking away for subtraction and ending up with a smaller number than the one I started with; it simply never occurred to me to compare two numbers and find the difference between them.

Another way to provoke teachers' thinking is to ask them to think about number sentences and ask whether firstly, they, and secondly, their pupils, would deem them to be possible or not. For example, they might 'know' that $5 = 4 + ?$ is permissible but predict that some of their pupils would disagree. This can provide a lively catalyst for discussion. Looking through the exam scripts of secondary pupils produces a host of other examples of misconceptions which could have been avoided had the mathematical foundations built in primary school been more substantial.

To summarise: there need to be at least three main aims in any in-service course focusing on subtraction:

- Ensuring that the teachers are confident about the basic concepts involved.
- Helping teachers appreciate the longer term value of providing their pupils with a thorough grounding in subtraction and highlighting some of the consequences if they fail to do so.
- Focusing attention on children's thinking, why they respond in the ways they do and why it is important for them to communicate their ideas clearly and confidently.

Communicating Related Follow-up Activities

Talking about and using subtraction in a wide variety of situations is an excellent way to broaden understanding. Subtraction can be easily incorporated into a wide range of topics with little effort. An obvious example is to use it in design and technology but it also fits comfortably into subjects such as history (life spans, dates and so on); geography (rainfall, temperatures, distances...); science (including astronomy where the distances between planets provide some testingly large numbers), and even religious education where one might be interested in thinking about dates before and after the Common Era. Less formal – but equally valid – opportunities can arise through activities and projects such as sports days, planning fêtes and making costumes for drama productions. If the tasks are subtly introduced then often even the most reluctant contributor in mathematics sessions will be calculating away without being hampered by the perception that they are poor mathematicians.

Summary of Key Ideas

- There is more to subtraction than simply taking away.
- Many people find subtraction complex and have a poor understanding of it.
- It is important that teachers and pupils share their mathematical thinking and come to value each others' strategies.
- In order to create sound foundations on which to build, primary teachers need to expose their pupils to opportunities to apply a range of subtraction structures.
- Subtraction can be incorporated into a wide range of relevant and realistic activities across the primary classroom.

Pause for Reflection

- Without referring to the chapter above, what subtraction structures do you recall?
- Take a moment to think about what you did yesterday: did you do any subtracting? What strategies did you use? (I suspect you did far more subtracting than you might have predicted. You could ask a colleague to predict how many times they subtract in a day; I think they might be surprised.)
- Why might teaching subtraction solely in terms of 'taking away' lead to difficulties in secondary school?
- Children do not always like to admit that they are, for example, 'shorter than', 'younger than', 'fatter than'. What activities can you think of that might encourage them to use such vocabulary without feeling awkward or inferior in any way?

Further Reading

Haylock, D.H. (2006) *Mathematics Explained for Primary Teachers* (3rd edition). London: Sage Publications.
     This is a very clear introduction to primary mathematics which covers the basic ideas surrounding subtraction in an amusing and informative way. Our students love it!

Hansen, A. (ed.) (2005) *Children's Errors in Mathematics: Understanding Common Misconceptions in the Primary School*. Exeter: Learning Matters.
     This is a very accessible book which describes children's misunderstandings and how they may have have arisen.

Cockburn, A.D. (1999) *Teaching Mathematics with Insight*. London: Falmer Press.
     If you wish to know more about the complexities surrounding the teaching and learning of subtraction, you might find this helpful.

References

Desforges, C. and Cockburn, A.D. (1987) *Understanding the Mathematics Teacher: A Study of Practice in the First School*. London: The Falmer Press.

Kamii, C. (1985) *Young Children Reinvent Arithmetic*. New York: Teachers College Press.

Endnotes

[1] Mrs R is a fictional character but the discussion is an amalgam of conversations observed in more than one classroom.

[2] When I first wrote that question I ended it with '... 5 children are absent. How many people are here today?' My reason for doing so was to avoid the use of children twice in such close proximity but, had I used 'people' rather than 'children', I was opening up the possibility of misunderstandings for a child might – entirely reasonably from their perspective – have responded '21', i.e. 20 children and 1 teacher.

[3] I was tempted to add '... for Jane?' but, had I done so, a child might have responded '3' working on the assumption that the remaining 6 would have been divided between me and Jane.

[4] N.B. When making the game it is important to ensure that the answers to each question are different otherwise two children might respond at once.

CHAPTER 2

Communicating Ideas about Space and Shape

Brigitte Spindeler and Bernd Wollring

Communicating the Theme

Lena: Those look nice. How did you make them?

Hanna: They seem a bit tricky at first. But once you see how it is done they are easy. I used a poster to help me.

John: How did you make this house, Jack?

Jack: It's hard to explain – but I can show you.

Communication about mathematics does not need to be through written or spoken words or symbols. Indeed, a person's understanding of space and shape may be substantially enhanced and improved by broadening the range of strategies and methods of communication. Figure 2.1 shows a poster made by Hanna.

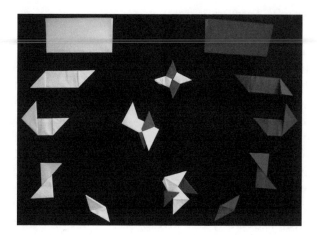

Figure 2.1   Hanna's poster

In this chapter we will demonstrate how children's appreciation of shape and space may develop significantly using forms and constructions as the basis for communication. We have found this approach to be especially fruitful for use in primary schools. The ability to reason and prove – which is important in more advanced mathematics – builds upon experiences and knowledge gained through constructing shapes and documentinging the process. The activities we discuss relate well to those in the revised National Numeracy Strategy.

Many topics focusing on two- and three-dimensional geometry in primary school are traditionally represented by two-dimensional drawings. But such an approach is not the only option and, indeed, it is not always the most appropriate. Primary children are rarely given the opportunity to use written descriptions of how to make objects. When they do, the work is seldom child-friendly or meaningful and often it is an artificial exercise or simply a means of assessing pupils' knowledge and understanding (such as in examinations).

Paper folding

Paper folding is a highly effective alternative to drawing and the written word when teaching shape and space. This method is particularly suitable for making symmetrical objects, as many of the activities stress the significance of line symmetry. Thus paper folding is not only a way of discovering the symmetrical properties of shapes but it can also assist in the construction of certain geometrical shapes.

Figure 2.2a   Typical BStars

Figure 2.2b   An SHouse

Documenting the process with Folding Posters

We have also found various highly successful ways in which children can exchange ideas and communicate their folding constructions. This may be done using documents we describe as 'Folding Posters' which children can read as well as create for themselves. In essence, they demonstrate the process of a construction by showing the intermediate steps of the folding process in a logical arrangement starting from the unfolded paper and ending with the completed folded object. Our experiences show that communicating via Folding Posters is not only appropriate and effective for 2-D folded objects but also works well with spatial 3-D ones. Moreover the posters turn out to be a powerful means of communication and they are particularly helpful for those children who have difficulty with written language.

Having worked in many primary classrooms with a range of children of all ages, we have found two objects that are particularly effective in promoting this approach – the 'BStar' and the 'SHouse'.

Communicating the Concepts

We believe that geometric shapes – including symmetry – are best introduced to primary children using specific objects. For example, line symmetry in 2-D shapes may be illustrated by the typical shape of a painted heart and rotational symmetry may be illustrated by the shape of windmill sails. However we propose two objects which both match, and extend, these criteria: the 'BStar' and the 'SHouse' shown in Figures 2.2a and 2.2b. The BStar is a starlet, assembled from two folded parts, which also appears in the Japanese literature on paper folding. We came across this idea in a kindergarten from a kind educator called Brigitte, and so we named the star after her. The SHouse was conceptualised by one of us – Bernd. It is assembled from four folded parts and a roof which is gently laid on top. The first child who folded it in a primary school was called Sara; so the SHouse is named after her.

2-D and 3-D

The BStar represents two-dimensional plane objects, although the folding demands spatial activities. The SHouse represents three-dimensional spatial objects. A lively impression of the objects is given by the video clips on the DVD accompanying this book. There you will also find some photos of the objects, the documents and classroom scenes (see DVD, Items 2.7 and 2.8).

Mathematical sense and material sense

BStar and SHouse were chosen and designed to demonstrate important mathematical features, namely line symmetry, rotational symmetry and geometric shapes, and the relationships between these features. We call this the 'mathematical sense'. Figure 2.3 shows the rotational symmetric BStar made from line symmetric parts. Figure 2.4 shows the symmetric spatial SHouse, assembled from symmetric parts.

These objects were chosen because, from a child's perspective, they are not obviously mathematical and they appear to relate to real life and thus support a literacy based approach. This we call the 'material sense', an expression which is only an approximate translation of the German word '*Werksinn*', which originates from the field of reform pedagogy ('*Reformpädagogik*'), meaning appealing to children rather than focusing on the mathematical aspects.

Figure 2.3 *Examples of line symmetry from the BStar*

Figure 2.4 *Symmetrical parts of the SHouse*

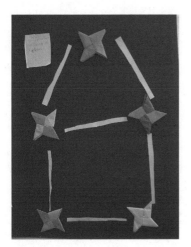

Figure 2.5 *Constellations of stars, made from different sized BStars*
Left: 'Cerberus' (pre-service teacher), Centre: 'The plough' (pupil, year 4), Right: 'Kepheus' (team of pupils, year 4)

BStars and SHouses make sense not only as single objects but also arranged together in groups. We call this their 'ensemble sense'. Complex objects which stimulate and develop children's ensemble sense include constellations made from BStars and villages made from SHouses.

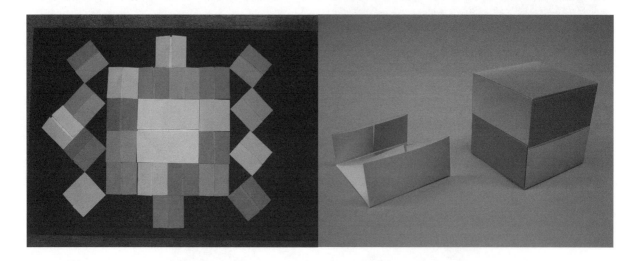

Figure 2.6a *Christmas calendar made from 24 different sized bases of SHouses*

Figure 2.6b *Cube made from eight bases of SHouses*

Figure 2.7 *Constructions made from SHouses: a village, towers and cubes*

Differentiation

The size of BStars and SHouses may be adjusted to make the folding more or less easy. The individual components of the SHouse can also be used to make other objects such as plane (flat) calendars and spatial cubes or towers.

Below we introduce the documents on the constructions – especially the Folding Posters – we think work best.

Communicating Experiences with Pre-service Teachers

The main point we want to make here is that it is important that pre-service teachers try paper folding themselves and reflect on its value before they start to work with pupils.

Pre- and in-service teachers may come on courses with different experiences of the geometry of paper folding. They may or may not have done it before, they may or may not have experienced different forms of communicating around the subject and they may or may not be able to predict children's experiences of paper folding. Taking this into account, you may adopt one of several approaches with student teachers.

Focus on exploring and folding

If the focus lies on folding geometric shapes and creating the objects then an investigative approach tends to be effective, especially if the pre-service teachers are not familiar with the objects and the folding techniques connected with them. Similarly, if the pre-service teachers have no previous experience of Folding Posters, it is a good idea if they begin by 'reading' – that is, exploring – the posters and then use them to make their own constructions. Having achieved this they might proceed to 'writing' – that is, making – their own Folding Posters. Figure 2.8 shows BStar Folding Posters created by year 2 pupils.

Figures 2.8   *Folding Posters showing how to make a BStar created by year 2 pupils*

Focus on documenting

If the focus lies more on communication aspects then 'writing' works well as a starting point and this means creating documents. One organisational option, for instance, is for two pre-service teachers to cooperate: the more practical one unfolds and refolds the objects while the other is busy creating a document, such as a Folding Poster for example.

Meta-analysis of documents

A further option is for the pre-service teachers to work on meta-tasks using documents. They analyse folding documents created by pupils or teachers, which may be Folding Posters or texts related to them. This might involve describing and analysing several posters at once and producing a mind map. This activity consists of arranging the Folding Posters, or reduced-size photos of them, by certain criteria and by comparing, evaluating and discussing the results of the comparisons.

Communicating Activities for the Classroom

The following activity relates to the focus on *reading and folding*.

Activity
Constructing BStars or SHouses from Folding Posters

1		Provide:	Either a photograph of or an original Folding Poster – or more if a choice is desirable
2	>	Exploring	Accept or choose a Folding Poster Read the Folding Poster (with eyes and hands)
3	>	Constructing	Follow the steps shown to make the object
4	>	Product	You have created your own BStar or SHouse
5		Documenting	Create a Folding Poster

Figure 2.9 shows year 3 children from the Czech Republic making BStars having read a poster, and Figure 2.10 shows year 2 children in Germany folding SHouses having read a poster. Here the focus in steps 2 and 3 of the activity lies on reading the posters, visually as well as in a tactile way. With the optional step 5 the students' abilities in evaluating and writing such documents are also initiated. The Folding Posters given to the children may vary in type and origin. Figures 2.8 to 2.11 show four examples of Folding Posters, two of them made by pupils from year two and the other two made by teachers with experience in this field.

To summarise, the BStar and SHouse are simple objects through which geometric ideas and concepts may be conveyed in a child-centred and purposeful way.

Figure 2.9   *Year 3 Czech children reading a poster and making BStars*

Figure 2.10   *Year 2 children reading a poster and making SHouses in Germany*

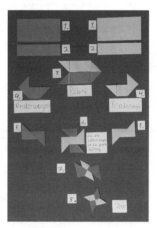

Figure 2.11   *BStar Folding Posters made by experienced primary school teachers*

We have observed four different ways to approach paper folding and the related geometry in the mathematics classroom, two traditional approaches and two influenced by a constructivist perspective.

Traditional Approach 1: Showing and imitating step by step

An expert – teacher or pupil – shows the folding step by step and, simultaneously, the pupils follow step by step.

Traditional Approach 2: Reading printed instructions and building

Printed instructions, typically copied from a specialised book, paper or from the internet, provide information for the pupils on how to create the objects.

The first approach provides few opportunities for discovery and differentiation. It may, be helpful in individual cases where support is needed. The second approach is difficult for some children as they are not always able to decode the necessary metric and spatial information from the 'instruction'. Often the texts from specialised books on paper folding imply certain iconic codes which one needs to know to understand the text. We suggest that this approach is more valid for revision or more advanced activities. Using constructivist approaches can avoid these disadvantages.

Constructivist Approach 1: Exploring an object and building a copy

The pupils get an object or several identical objects to disassemble and unfold. They are then expected to reconstruct the object by folding a copy.

Constructivist Approach 2: Reading Folding Posters and building

The pupils get a Folding Poster and are asked to create the documented object.

The following activity relates to the focus on exploring and folding:

Activity
Folding BStar or SHouse by exploring an already folded object

1		Provided	BStar or SHouse as pattern (has to be returned to the teacher at the end of the session)
2	>	Exploring	Disassemble the object and unfold the parts
3	>	Constructing	Fold by copying the parts and assembling
4	>	Product	Own BStar or SHouse.
5		Documenting	Create a (fleetingly arranged) Folding Poster

Figure 2.12   *Year 3 children making a BStar poster in the UK*

We suggest that pupils cooperate in pairs or in teams of four so they can exchange ideas and support each other. Each group gets one or two objects as patterns which they will later return to the teacher. We have found that giving back the patterns emphasises that the created objects are the personal product and property of the pupils, which they may keep and take home. (If the paper colour of the patterns is different from that of the paper the pupils use to create their own objects it is easy to see which objects have to be given back.)

At the beginning of the exploration the pupils should learn to disassemble the objects into their parts and to re-assemble them:

2.1 >	Exploring	Disassemble the object into parts and then re-assemble it
2.2 >	Exploring	Disassemble the parts and unfold them for reconstruction

The reconstruction of the BStar involves a special challenge as re-assembling the parts involves rotating one piece in relation to another. This is a complex spatial activity.

In our classroom trials some pupils spontaneously folded several BStars as soon as they had matched the first one. Nearly all of those who did not match this in the classroom matched it at home. They took home the given pattern or even a BStars which other children gave them as a gift. Some pupils spontaneously folded BStars of various sizes from differently-sized squares of paper. Some later created star constellations with their BStars which was a pleasing application and which produced an attractive display (see Figure 2.5). Other pupils hung the BStars from the classroom ceiling. Ensembles like these have a lot of aesthetic appeal.

We observed that some pupils tended to take apart the objects and unfold the parts completely. Some were then unable to recreate the BStar, so we gave them two BStars to provide a finished model as a visual aid. This problem is less serious with the SHouse as it has two gable walls, so one part can remain folded.

It can be very helpful to ask the pupils to put both the unfolded and folded pieces into the middle of the table in a sequence to show the process of construction (see Figure 2.13). Documenting the process with this logical step-by-step arrangement is the key objective in working with Folding Posters. It is the crucial aid in understanding rich and complex visual and tactile information about a process which for pupils of this age, and even for adults in general, is hard to grasp using spoken or written language. Figure 2.12 shows year 3 pupils from the UK 'writing' (making) a poster for the BStar. Figure 2.13 illustrates the stages 'on the way to the Folding Poster'.

Figures 2.13   *'On the way to the Folding Poster: Fleeting folding documents of the BStar and the SHouse*

Figures 2.14   *Isabella, Jennifer and Volkan (year 4) making, altering and proudly displaying their BStar folding poster*

We limited the poster size to 50 x 70 cm and the size of the paper squares for folding to 15 x 15 cm. The pupils therefore had to choose which pieces to put on the poster as there was not enough space to include every single step in the folding process; not always an easy task for some children as they wanted to include every step on their poster! Sometimes we noticed that the process of making a poster could be enriched by asking pupils to identify 'difficult steps' and suggesting that they might wish to insert additional pieces to explain these steps.

The exercise produces rich and sometimes lengthy discussions among the pupils about which pieces to include on their posters. The negotiations can be complex and involve much discussion about space and shape. By asking small groups of children or pairs to create their own posters in numerous classrooms over the years, we have acquired a wide variety of Folding Posters.

The Folding Posters are not 2-D documents like printed instructions; rather they have an added tactile dimension. You might ask that each part on the poster can be unfolded so that it looks like the preceding part. This may not always be possible but it focuses the pupils' attention on the need to consider the relationships between the constituent parts of the Folding Poster. Figure 2.14 shows Isabella, Jennifer and Volkan – year 4 German pupils – 'writing' a BStar Folding Poster. In discussion they decide to change the arrangement of the text. By not sticking down the various elements of the poster, the pupils are able to move the parts around giving a framework to the discussion.

Figure 2.15 shows Jonatan and Elias – also year 4 pupils – reading the Folding Poster designed by Isabella, Jennifer and Volkan, and then building a BStar using it.

Figure 2.15 *Jonaton and Elias (year 4) reading the folding poster designed by Isabella, Jennifer and Volkan and using it to build BStars*

Audience-specific

Folding Posters can be designed for specific audiences, perhaps for pupils in another class, for younger children or even adults! Sometimes you might suggest that pupils add labels with written texts or numbers. We suggest that these are not written directly onto the poster but rather put on separate pieces of paper which may be moved around the poster, like the folded parts, during the discussion.

Fleeting versus fixed

Before the constituent parts of a poster have been stuck down the poster is called a 'fleeting document' of the folding process. When the pupils have reached a consensus the parts are glued onto the poster as they agreed: it is now a 'fixed document'. To maximise the benefits of cooperative working the gluing stage should be towards the end of the lesson, leaving the option to move, add or take away parts for as long as possible.

Global shape

Not only do such discussions encourage children to reflect on the meaning of the single steps, it can also bring out the importance of the whole construction – 'the global shape' – of the Folding Poster. For example some posters are arranged in lines or columns, like written text. Others reflect the symmetrical nature of the BStar folding process (see Figure 2.11).

Many strategies – open documents

The folding of the parts of the SHouse can be documented by Folding Posters similar to those for the BStar (see DVD, Items 2.3 and 2.4). The gable wall, however, allows for various folding options which all fit the SHouse (see Figure 2.16). These may come to light if the folding poster does not clearly demonstrate whether certain folds are 'valley-folds' or 'mountain-folds'. Using paper of two different colours helps to show how different strategies yield different gable patterns.

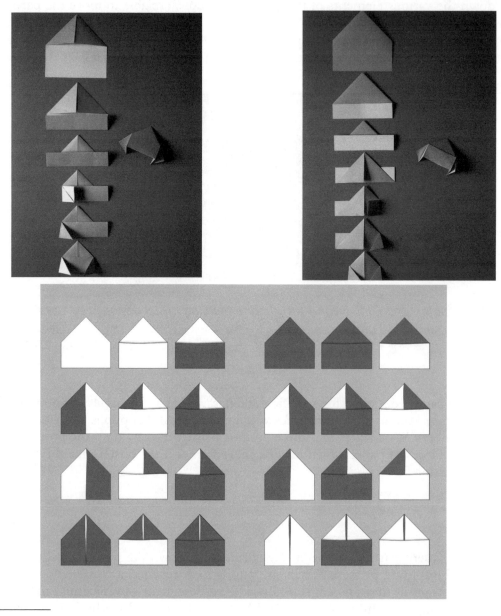

Figures 2.16   *SHouse: Folding Posters for the gable wall with different folding options*

Spatial documents for spatial objects

The SHouse is a spatial object so it is difficult to document its construction using 2-D folding posters. Photos may help but, as Figures 2.13 to 2.17 show, children sometimes find their own methods for documenting spatial construction using a spatial Folding Poster. The spatial Folding Poster shows, as the pupils said, 'a little village of SHouses which are under construction' (see Figure 2.17). The different houses are at different stages of construction.

Figure 2.17   Spatial Folding Poster showing the spatial construction of SHouses

Although Folding Posters tend to be constructed in similar ways they show a lot of individuality; each one documents the perceptions of those who made it. From our point of view, the individuality of the process and resulting documents is a very important experience for pupils with respect to mathematical activities as a whole.

Presentations and exhibitions

Ensembles made from BStars and SHouses – for instance constellations or models of villages – are very appropriate for displays within the classroom and throughout the school. We think you'll find that, by including the Folding Posters as well, many others will embark on construction tasks!

Communicating Ideas for In-service Courses

We have found two different approaches to in-service teacher training to be particularly effective:

- Teachers' activities corresponding to pupils' activities in creating and documenting.
- Teachers exploring and assessing documents to enlarge their basis of deciding and planning.

Teachers' activities corresponding to pupils' activities in creating and documenting

If folding paper objects and documenting their construction using Folding Posters is new for the participating teachers their activities will be similar to those for the pupils. The intention is that the teachers will both experience the task for themselves whilst reflecting on the process as a potential mathematical exercise for their pupils.

We have found that it works best if teachers make copies of given objects (for example an SHouse) in an explorative way and then think about how they might document or develop their work. To introduce the idea of Folding Posters, then, you may – as with pupils – explain the concept using a different object to the one that the teachers have just folded.

At first glance teachers may consider the Folding Posters rather complicated and elaborate but, with experience of them, they generally find them to be effective documents. The contrast between the capacity of Folding Posters and spoken communication or written texts can be elicited by an elementary communication experiment in which a simple folding procedure consisting of not more than two or three steps (for instance the first three steps of folding the gable wall of the SHouse) has to be communicated without using hands, pictures or materials but merely by a spoken (or written) instruction. This has proved to be a successful way to start a workshop with teachers.

Activity:
An experiment to compare verbal instructions and Folding Posters

Person A stands and folds a certain simple object

Person B is standing facing person A and has to keep his/her hands behind them

The rest of the teachers stand in a group behind person A and facing person B

Now person B has to describe to the group, without using his/her hands, but in words only, person A's folding actions (which the group cannot see) so that they too can produce a similar folded object

---

In addition you may decide whether the group members may ask person B questions or not

---

This experiment shows how difficult it is to discuss geometric constructions using spoken language even if they can be readily constructed. However, as we have demonstrated, constructing objects and presenting the process using folding posters is an excellent, stress-free way to develop geometrical language.

On seeing a range of posters you may conclude that there is an optimal Folding Poster for a given object. In this case, as we discuss below, comparing different posters can be a useful exercise.

Teachers exploring and assessing folding documents to enlarge their basis of deciding and planning.

Here we assume that the participating teachers are experienced with paper folding in the mathematics classroom and therefore we suggest that they deal with meta-tasks concerning the comparing, describing and assessing of Folding Posters.

The first aim is to make the teachers aware of the basic idea of variety: as with many mathematical tasks we are aiming for a specific outcome but the ways to reach this solution may differ. This is less true for the processes of folding – although some variety may appear – but it is certainly the case when creating posters. As mentioned above, no two Folding Posters are exactly the same. In our trials we have found certain types of posters but never two which were completely identical.

To prepare the teachers for making decisions and organising the classroom activities, we suggest you take a given set of Folding Posters or photos of them and explore, describe, sort and classify them using different criteria and, in so doing, assess them with respect to their effectiveness. Figure 2.18 shows various types of Folding Posters for the BStar, some made by pupils and others by pre-service teachers.

Figures 2.18 *Various types of BStar Folding Posters made by pupils and pre-service teachers*

In the classroom this can be done using Folding Posters created by the pupils. The advantage of this is that the work is genuine but the disadvantage is that inexperienced teachers may judge the work too harshly, which can be very de-motivating for the seemingly less successful children. Similarly it can decrease the motivation of all other pupils if the teacher presents a certain poster as his/her favourite poster, especially if the assessment was done primarily for aesthetic reasons rather than for functionality. For example, some of the less attractive Folding Posters may constitute very effective instructions from which many pupils may work successfully. The opposite can also hold true.

Therefore as a third activity we recommend a systematic comparative analysis of Folding Posters and for this we recommend the set of 21 photos of posters on the DVD (Item 2.5), some of which were created by year 4 pupils and some by pre-service teachers.

Mind maps on the meta-level

To analyse the Folding Posters the same principle holds as for their construction and again mind maps are used. The posters are mind maps made from folded parts, and the position of each part expresses its relationships to other parts. Here the complete Folding Posters play the same role as the folded parts played before: the inter-relationships are represented in the same sense by the way they are arranged with respect to each other in the mind map. This arranging determines our third activity for teachers. The activity can be done according to a range of criteria and it may be accompanied by various questions which are presented and discussed in more detail below.

Activity: Meta-tasks on Folding Posters
Describing, analysing, comparing and assessing

Material: Set or selection of Folding Posters for the same folded object

M1   Arrange the folding posters in a mind map by one of the following criteria:

    C1 Organisation and direction of reading written text.

    C2 Use of colours: decorative versus functional

    C3 Overall impression of poster ('Gestalt')

    C4 Resolution, density of documentation: number of folded pieces to elicit certain folding steps

    C5 Correct shape of parts, correct positions of parts?

    C6 Who made the poster: pupils, teachers, pre-service teachers, artists?

    C7 Expected success for certain audience groups

M2   Folding Poster: Find any errors and suggest corrections

M3   Folding Poster: Put forward ideas for re-arranging. Reasons?

M4   Folding Poster: Predict reconstruction success. Reasons?

M5   Folding Poster: Create screening tasks (Reconstruct screened parts)

C1 How and in which directions is the poster to be read? What written texts are there? Are they necessary to understand the poster?

C2 Are the colours chosen chaotically or just to make the poster look nice? Did the authors cooperate? Or are the colours chosen in a functional way and do they help the construction process? Is the construction of the same part encoded in the same colour?

C3 Does the poster express a general construction principle or not?

C4 Does the poster include a high number of steps or just a few? If the poster includes a high number, is it necessarily a better poster? Which posters are better at indicating difficulties?

C5 Are all the folding steps encoded correctly? If not, can the poster be understood in spite of that?

C6 Are the authors of the posters identifiable? Are there special features indicating authors from special age groups or from special person groups?

C7 *The crucial question*: Which posters do you think will be successful in the sense that the addressees know what they need to do? Figure 2.19 shows some Folding Posters classified by a primary teacher in terms of 'very readable', 'readable', 'partially readable', 'not readable', 'other'.

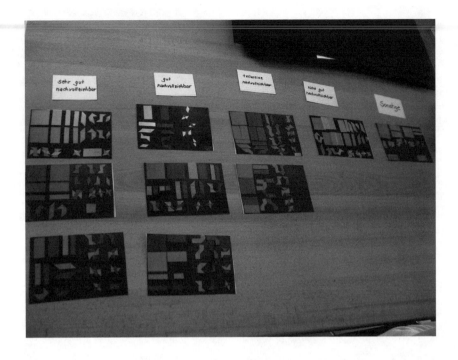

Figure 2.19   *Classification of some Folding Posters by readability, arranged by a primary school teacher. (Translation from the German: 'very readable', 'readable', 'partially readable', 'not readable', 'others')*

Screening tasks

In connection with mind maps we find 'screening tasks' to be a very useful activity. A screening task is where you present someone with a Folding Poster which has a piece missing (this is usually done by covering a particular part of the poster). The aim of the exercise is to reconstruct the hidden – or screened – part in a mind map by making inferences based on the parts near to it that are still visible. Such an exercise is very similar to those where a child is given an incomplete text and asked to fill in the missing words or to complete a calculation in which some numbers are omitted.

Screening tasks serve two purposes: firstly, they are a useful tool for pre- and in-service teachers to assess the internal consistency and the logical flow of Folding Posters and, secondly, they constitute an informative and rewarding task for pupils. More specifically, if done with effective Folding Posters they support the exploration of the folding process, with faulty posters they help to find mistakes, and with redundant posters they help to identify parts which are not necessary. They also provide you with tools to explore both the folding process and folding documents. Figure 2.20 shows parts of a poster hidden from view and Figure 2.21 shows the 'solution' of a screening task.

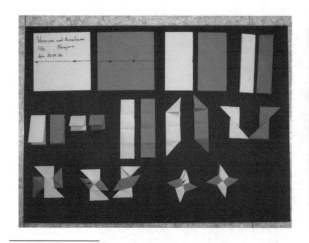 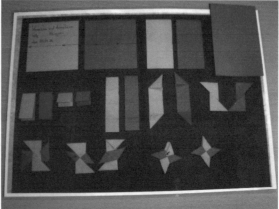

Figure 2.20   *Hiding parts of a Folding Poster*

Figure 2.21   *Showing the 'missing parts' in a screening task*

Figure 2.21 shows screening being used to explore the concept of symmetry: the hidden part on the BStar Folding Poster may be reconstructed by examining the preceding and succeeding parts in the process, or by referring to its symmetric partner if this is documented.

Communication among groups

Finally, we introduce an activity based on the exchange of documents. Again it emphasises communicating strategies and we have found that it works well with both teacher and pupil groups. These activities do not require groups to be together physically, as they can also be conducted via 'mailed documents'.

Activity: Groups cooperate by exchanging documents

(Documents may be about the same object or different ones)

1A   Preparation: Group A explores folded object A, copies it and documents the process by making Folder Poster A

1B   Preparation: Group B explores folded object B, copies it and documents the process by making Folding Poster B

2   The groups exchange posters

3A   Group A creates object B using Folding Poster B and evaluates the poster

3B   Group B creates object A using Folding Poster A and evaluates the poster

4   The groups discuss their Folding Posters by correspondence

**Activity: Groups cooperate
by exchanging re-worked documents or comments**

(Documents may be about the same object or different ones)

1A   Preparation: Group A reads given Folding Poster A, folds object A and re-works or gives comments on Folding Poster A

1B   Preparation: Group B reads given Folding Poster B, folds object B and re-works or gives comment on Folding Poster B

2   The groups exchange the Folding Posters.

3A   Group A folds object B using Folding Poster B and evaluates Folding Poster B

3B   Group B folds object A using Folding Poster A and evaluates Folding Poster A

4   The groups correspond about their Folding Posters

Communicating Related Follow-up Activities

The activities introduced here raise the question of how to begin. Should the exploration of the geometry of a folded object be started by analysing a given piece as a pattern to be copied, or via a document in the sense of a Folding Poster? Making an object and working on documents, however, are complementary activities. So as a consequence the following question arises:

How can we reach reasonable closed cycles of working which entail both making objects and documenting the process?

One strategy we suggest has the advantage that the children analyse the object guided by an aim. It has the disadvantage that they may lose an overview and abandon the process. Keeping the overview can be supported by a document, even by a fleeting one.

A second strategy we suggest has the advantage that by using a document children have an overview at any time, and therefore they can correct mistakes and restart if necessary. It has the disadvantage that the children are in general less motivated to 'write' a Folding Poster on the same object when they already have a good poster. To initiate the re-writing of a poster you need to be very careful in your choice of the poster you give them. We have found that the highest motivation for re-writing comes when a poster is full of the wrong pieces or pieces in the wrong order or position.

To reach reasonable closed cycles of work we have found these follow-up activities to be effective.

Evaluating Folding Posters and transferring posters to another object

An activity you might like to try is to ask your class to *evaluate a Folding Poster and then*, for instance, send a letter to its creators. You might stress that they should single out aspects of the poster for praise and indicate places where it is difficult to read. They might also make suggestions as to what could be changed. As another follow-up activity, having used a Folding Poster the children create another poster for the same or a different object and then 'transfer' or send it to another working group.

Transferring the idea of the poster to other objects

Give the children a folded-paper object as a pattern to be copied and ask them to make a document of this activity. Support this by giving them a Folding Poster demonstrating the folding of an object different from the one they are working with. The children should begin to understand the 'grammar' of the Folding Posters through the poster you have given them. The object documented by this poster should be simple and not too complicated.

Summary of Key Ideas

- *Paper folding.* Paper folding opens up shape and space to all primary school children. This process is activity-based and also encourages language to emerge. Two- and three-dimensional objects are accessible by paper folding techniques.
- *The objects.* The BStar and the SHouse are very effective ways to represent geometric concepts but they may be replaced by other objects. They encourage mathematical sense, material sense ('*Werksinn*') and ensemble sense. Both objects are appropriate for the primary school classroom.
- *The BStar.* The BStar is a two-dimensional object which has rotational symmetry and may be assembled from two parts which are line symmetrical to each other. Creating the BStar is a mini-course on line symmetry.
- *The SHouse.* The SHouse is spatial and assembled from five parts, some of which may be identical. The SHouse and the component parts have two- and three-dimensional symmetries.
- *Documents.* An essential and fundamental aspect of geometry consists in creating 'plans', that is documenting shapes and constructions.

- *The documents: Folding Posters*. In addition to discussion and exploration, Folding Posters are an effective means for communicating about paper folding geometry. Primary school children can read folding posters and they can 'write' them. We have observed that the quality of communication using Folding Posters is largely independent of the pupils' language abilities; written language is not necessary. Folding Posters may be created within groups, thus stimulating and developing language.
- *Geometry in primary school*. Geometry deals with shape and space 'gestalt' and symmetries. It is an integral and fundamental part of primary school mathematics. A well thought through and fully integrated introduction to shape and space in primary school leads to a rich and broad understanding of mathematics in general and geometry in particular.
- *Mathematics within the network of topics*. Stars yield constellations, models of houses lead to villages. Both may be coupled with descriptions and stories. In these ways networks are created between primary mathematics, language education and the humanities.

Pause for Reflection

- Just think for a moment: what shape is a star? How do children draw stars? Are BStars the same shape as the stars children draw naturally?
- How do you fold a regular octagon?
- Does paper folding help you and your pupils to explore line symmetry?
- Does the work with the folded stars and houses fit into other curriculum areas besides mathematics?
- Might the work with the posters have cross-curricular applications?
- What potential do you see in the screening tasks?
- Do you think that assembling the BStar or the SHouse includes specific difficulties? Why might this be the case?
- Do you think that paper folding and Folding Posters might encourage the more reluctant and less confident to engage in – and even enjoy – mathematical activities?
- Do you think that paper folding activities might encourage more cooperation between pupils or between teachers?
- Are the activities we suggest compatible with the standards presented in the National Numeracy Strategy?

Material sets

We suggest that you prepare the following materials for both teacher training courses and classroom use (DVD, Item 2.1): One set contains activity-cards (DVD, item 2.2), 21 photo-cards (size A5) and 4 photo-cards (size A4) of Folding Posters for the BStar (DVD, item 2.5), mini-posters (size A4) for the SHouse (DVD, item 2.4), and additional information on symmetry for teachers (DVD, item 2.6). You will find files on the accompanying DVD (items 2.1–2.8). We recommend that you add at least two complete folded BStars, some folded materials for the SHouse – especially the gables, and any further material you think you might require.

Further Reading

British Origami Society www.britishorigami.org.uk, www.britishorigami.info

This is a clear and well-structured site detailing the activities of the British Origami Society, ranging from simple examples to advanced ones. There is an extra section focusing on paper folding in the classroom.

Durkin, K. and Shire, B. (eds) (1991) *Language in Mathematical Education: Research and Practice.* Buckingham: Open University Press.

This is a basic text on the role of language in mathematics education.

Fusé, T. (1990) *Unit Origami.* Tokyo and New York: Japan Publications Inc.

This is a classic monograph on paper folding. The special accent is on modular origami i.e. on origami objects which are made from several folded pieces that fit into each other.

Gallin, P. and Ruf, U. (1999) *Dialogisches Lernen in Sprache und Mathematik. Band 1: Austausch unter Ungleichen.* Seelze: Kallmeyersche Verlagsbuchhandlung.

Origami Deutschland www.papierfalten.de

This is comparable with the homepage of the British Origami Society in Germany.

Origami USA www.origami-usa.org

This is comparable with the homepage of the British Origami Society in the United States of America.

CHAPTER 3

Constructing and Connecting 2-D and 3-D Shapes

Diana Hunscheidt and Andrea Peter-Koop

Communicating the Theme

> Seven-year-old Kylie knows the name for a square.
>
> However, as she had just been doing 3-D shapes in school,
>
> when she was shown a square and asked to name it
>
> she replied, 'It's a square ... no, we call it a cube in school'.

The introduction of the names of 2-D and 3-D shapes is frequently based on pictures of different shapes in our environment. While this usually works well with 2-D shapes, some children tend to get confused when 2-D illustrations of 3-D shapes are used instead of real objects or 3-D models; a 2-D illustration of a 3-D shape does not necessarily match with the child's mental image of the shape. It requires certain spatial skills to recognise a 2-D representation of a 3-D shape. In order to develop these skills learners need the opportunity to investigate 3-D objects or models: How many sides does a cube have? What do they look like? Are they all the same? How does it look when I view it from the side, from the top, from the bottom left ...? How do I have to turn it so that it looks like the cube in this picture?

In order to recognise a 2-D image of a cube children have to relate the image to the concrete object and its specific features. While many children learn to do this quite easily others tend to struggle. Being able to distinguish the names of 2-D and 3-D shapes is clearly important in mathematics; however, the ability to interpret 2-D images of 3-D shapes is even more important and is a challenge that we often have to face in our daily lives. Doctors, for example, must be able to understand an ultrasound picture, builders need to be able to read an architect's drawing.

Even young children encounter construction manuals when trying to assemble a new Lego® toy or the figure in a Kinder Surprise. Often such plans are discarded quickly because children fail to understand how they relate to the real object. Trial and error seems to be more promising than using the plan. Most adults who have ever tried to assemble furniture by using the instructions will relate to the frustration young children experience!

When it comes to teaching shape and space, therefore, one of the key questions we need to consider is how we can support children with the development of the spatial skills that they need?

- to distinguish between 2-D and 3-D shapes; and
- to relate iconic (that is, pictorial) representations to concrete objects or models.

The computer program BlockCAD is an ideal way to support the teaching and learning of spatial skills in primary mathematics in this context. It introduces children to the relationship between 3-D objects and their 2-D representations and enables them to develop their appreciation of key concepts through the medium of ICT. It is a freeware program developed by a Swedish professional programmer and self-declared 'Lego lover', Anders Issakson. Originally he developed the program for his own children and made it available through the internet. You can download BlockCAD if you go to: http://user.tninet.se/~hbh828t/anders.htm

BlockCAD is easily accessible to young learners. Lego-like blocks can be selected from a toolbox (see the right hand side of Figure 3.1) using mouse clicks. They can then be positioned in virtual buildings or objects. When encountering the program children tend to be fascinated by the inexhaustible supply of building blocks that BlockCAD provides. The fact that they can choose any of the given colours for each block and even add their own colour preferences to the colour options contributes to the attraction of the program. However, for classroom use, you might find it necessary to limit the supply of blocks and colour options so that pupils can concentrate on constructing rather than decorating! BlockCAD easily allows these options and therefore supports a great diversity of different constructions and themes. Eight-year-old Matti, when introduced to BlockCAD in year 3 maths class, commented, 'This is cool. Finally, I can have all the blocks I want in all the colours as many times as I need them!'

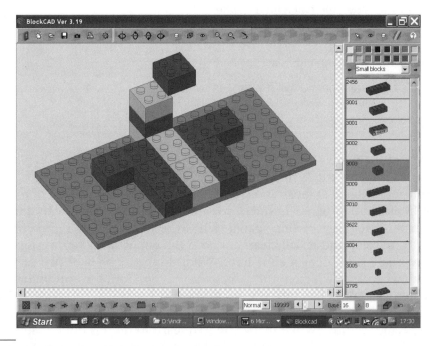

Figure 3.1 *Screenshot of a virtual construction in progress*

We have also observed that young girls, who often seem to prefer role playing to (technical) construction activities, are attracted to BlockCAD. They quickly make use of the colour options by choosing all shades of pink, orange and purple for the blocks they use – in exploration phases we saw many Barbie houses and cars.

The fact that ICT activities in general have a huge motivational factor for children also contributes to the easy acceptance of the program by primary pupils.

Like a professional construction program, BlockCAD offers continuously variable views of the object being made. Arrow icons in the menu make it very easy for the user to rotate the object. Many times younger children have said that they particularly like the program because the entire menu is based on symbols that are easy to explore and understand. In other words, the use of BlockCAD is not restricted by individual language and reading skills.

Try experimenting with the program and discover all its features and options. For a quick access and overview, Item 3.1 on the DVD accompanying this book offers an introduction to, and detailed explanation of, the program features. In summary, BlockCAD allows the child to construct objects with Lego-like blocks of varying complexity, investigate these objects on the screen through rotation, view the object from different perspectives, and make and print pictures of the self-created object.

In this chapter we will explain the underlying concepts involved in visualisation and orientation. We then demonstrate how these key aspects of shape and space in particular may be introduced and developed across the primary years through the use of the construction program BlockCAD.

Communicating the Concepts

The development of increasingly complex spatial skills is highlighted throughout the National Curriculum. In this section we will explain how the use of BlockCAD in the primary mathematics classroom,

- enables an innovative approach to the teaching and learning of space and shape;
- relates the learning about space and shape to children's experiences at play prior to, and out of, school;
- fosters alternative ways of communication in the classroom;
- complies with the ICT standards of the National Curriculum.

The example of Kylie at the beginning of the chapter illustrates how misunderstandings frequently arise when young children are first introduced to two- and three-dimensional shapes. In particular, problems occur when 3-D shapes are represented in 2-D in books and so on. For younger children the relationship between a 3-D object and its 2-D image is not always easy to understand. Classroom activities are frequently limited by the material available (for example construction kits, Plasticine), children's motor skills (for example joining straws or elastics when making solid shapes) and primary pupils' drawing abilities.

It is important to note that young children's drawings of 3-D shapes differ from the standard 2-D representations based on perspective drawing (see Lewis, 1963). When asked to draw a cube on which a door had been painted on the front side and a window on each of the two adjacent sides as in Figure 3.2a, primary children demonstrated the strategies shown in Figure 3.2b.

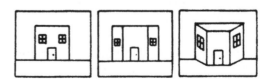

Figure 3.2a *Perspective drawing of the cube used by Lewis (1963)*

Figure 3.2b *Children's drawing strategies*

They drew

- only one side with all three features;
- a non-perspective drawing showing the three sides and their individual features; or
- tried to demonstrate their developing insight in perspective drawing by showing four sides of the cube but from an impossible point of perspective.

It is perhaps not surprising that such drawings can lead to confusion about the properties of the shape and structure of objects during classroom discussions; working with children's drawings clearly has some limitations. In this chapter we describe how generating pictures using a computer program might both support the development of children's drawing strategies and prevent some of the difficulties that such pictures present.

BlockCAD allows children to visualise and to experiment with 3-D objects in 2-D, and to create 2-D representations of 3-D objects based on perspective drawing. The created views can easily be printed out as screen shots in order to allow for their comparison and analysis. Moreover there is the added advantage that self-created objects can be viewed from different perspectives. This enables children to compare the effects that a change of view-point has on the image of the object and to relate iconic representations to a specific view-point. Figure 3.3, for example, shows images of the same object – a multicoloured pyramid – from three different perspectives.

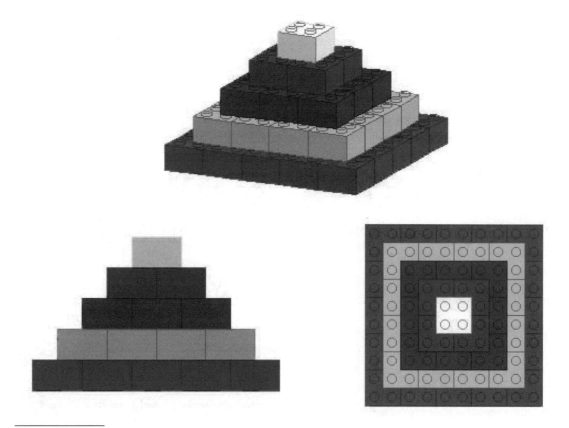

Figures 3.3 *Pyramid: 3 different perspectives*

To summarise, the computer environment provides an innovative approach to teaching space and shape. We have also observed that it fosters a deeper understanding of the relationship between 3-D objects and their 2-D representations.

Although BlockCAD is not deliberately aimed for use in the classroom, it has proven to be a very suitable tool for the teaching and learning of space and shape. The close connection to Lego and similar building activities makes it easily accessible for most children – even if they are not familiar with Lego blocks as such – and relates their mathematics learning to their experiences at play, both prior to and out of school.

The combination of play and school mathematics is seen as a way to help children realise and experience the close connection of mathematical knowledge and everyday activities as well as the importance and value of out-of-school experiences for their school mathematics learning. By combining the computer program (the virtual learning environment) with the use of building blocks (the real learning environment) BlockCAD-based learning environments offer individual challenges for mixed-ability classrooms. On the one hand, learners can be challenged to recreate concrete buildings/objects (of varying complexity provided by you or made by a classmate) in a virtual environment. While, on the other hand, you or a fellow pupil might introduce a virtual object as a BlockCAD file and ask a child to recreate it as a real object.

In both cases the question arises, 'What do I need to know and find out about the building/object in order to create its virtual (or real) counterpart?' Properties such as number, size and colour of blocks and their position within the structure have to be identified. Children will quickly discover that not all virtual constructions can be made into real objects because the virtual environment allows 'free-hanging' blocks that are not attached to any other block in the construction. When constructing with real blocks gravity obviously does not allow such structures! We have also frequently observed children moving forward and leaning over a screen in order to look at the back of a virtual object and then laughing when they realised that all they could see was the back of the computer and some cables.

Construction tasks in a combined virtual/real environment can also involve virtual building or disassembling using subassemblies as shown in Figures 3.4a and 3.4b for example.

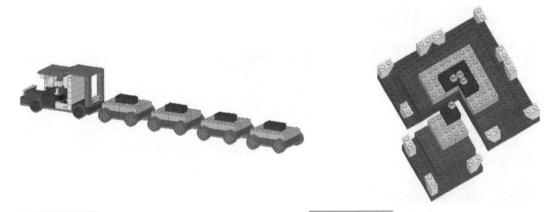

Figure 3.4a Train construction with subassemblies

Figure 3.4b Pyramid construction with subassembly

A feature that emphasises BlockCAD's similarity to professional graphics programs is the 'group concept'. BlockCAD allows the use of 'temporary groups' and 'subassemblies'. Temporary groups can be generated by selecting several blocks successively. The selected group can be re-positioned and then 'un-groups' automatically. A selected group can be saved as a subassembly for repeated use in a variety of constructions (see Item 3.1 on the DVD for further details).

The international exchange of classroom materials in the COSIMA project highlighted another key aspect of ICT assisted learning of space and shape. Properties and characteristics of buildings/objects created by German pupils could be easily communicated to pupils in the UK and the Czech Republic (and vice versa), despite their different native languages, through entirely iconic 'construction plans' (see Figures 3.5a and 3.5b).

Figure 3.5a   *Tower construction*

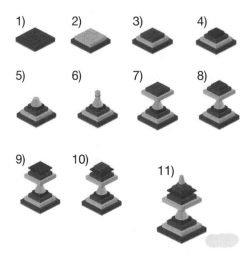

Figure 3.5b   *Construction plan for the tower*

Construction plans carry all the necessary information for the construction or re-construction of a building/object. Although their production is a highly mathematical process children find it very enjoyable and relevant. In order to generate a construction plan, they have to analyse the geometrical properties of the building/object and decide which views carry the necessary information. Different views and construction stages can easily be saved as JPG-files and then copied into text files (for details see Item 3.1 on the DVD). In our experience children quickly understood the procedures necessary for this process because they are very similar to standard word processing applications. We also found that children started to see connections to the construction manuals attached to new Lego and other toys. The fact that their own plan looked similarly professional to the industrial products made them feel proud and competent. Hand-drawn plans clearly would not have the same effect: firstly many children would find them almost impossible to produce due to lack of motor skills and drawing techniques and, secondly, their appearance would immediately identify them as children's products. While there is clearly nothing wrong with that at all, the fact that children can use a tool that produces professional looking images proved to be a great stimulus for the primary children we have worked with.

Such tasks employ substantial mathematical activities such as:

- making shapes and solids (both real and virtual);
- relating solid shapes to pictures of them, identifying different views and perspectives;
- recognising line symmetry (or the absence of it) and using this knowledge; for the construction plans.

The children's limited drawing skills and strategies, however, did not present a restriction to the effective communication of their knowledge and insights. (We certainly do not want to argue that learning activities in space and shape should generally be language free. Examples of how to challenge children to verbalise their observations are provided in the section 'Communicating Activities for the Classroom'.)

In this sense, the use of BlockCAD complies with the ICT standards of the National Curriculum. While the motivational benefit with respect to the use of ICT in classrooms is certainly an important issue, BlockCAD is a good example of how the careful selection and reflected implementation of ICT can help to extend children's mathematical understanding and communication. In many cases, children expressed surprise that they 'were not doing maths in a maths lesson'. They instead perceived their (highly mathematical) activities as playing and we certainly talked about that in class. This 'play approach' was particularly effective for the weaker learners – both in terms of their motivation and their learning outcomes. 'Playing' with BlockCAD transformed the program into a powerful tool for mathematics learning.

In summary, with respect to mathematical concepts and activities that can be explored using BlockCAD, the following curriculum areas can be covered in the learning environments that have been developed and trialled in the COSIMA project:

- Investigating the properties of real and virtual objects, for example:
  - How many blocks are used for the construction (make a bill of materials)?
  - Can the object be dismantled in subassemblies?
  - Which lines of symmetry can be found?
- Constructing real and virtual objects with pre-specified mathematical properties.
- Relating 2-D construction plans to 3-D objects.
- Developing construction plans in order to communicate the structure of given or self-constructed objects.
- Fostering of visualisation skills.

Communicating Experiences with Pre-service Teachers

When student teachers – just like primary pupils – are first introduced to BlockCAD they immediately associate their experiences with Lego.

Oh, this is cool. I loved playing with Lego when I was a kid. I have never seen it as a computer program.

Most of our student teachers have not encountered BlockCAD before when we start using it in methods courses. In many cases they do not link BlockCAD with mathematics learning as the following comment suggests:

I thought we were evaluating maths software, Ms Hunscheidt.

Hence, we are presented with the challenge of stimulating and supporting our student teachers' discovery of the opportunities BlockCAD presents with respect to the teaching and learning of space and shape. We usually introduce the work in three stages:

- Exploring the program.
- Anticipating and analysing pupils' solutions.
- Developing and trialling learning environments.

Figure 3.6   *Student teachers exploring BlockCAD*

Exploring the program

In order to introduce BlockCAD we frequently start with an exploration of the program's features by setting introductory problems such as:

> Set the base plate to 15 x 20 and build a one storey house using no more than three different colours.

One solution to this task is shown in Figure 3.7.

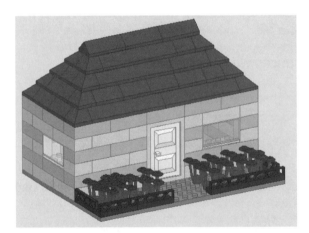

Figure 3.7   *BlockCAD house*

By solving a straightforward, relatively simple task the student teachers not only discover key features fairly quickly, they also experience some of the problems and limitations of the program. However, most of these – such as placing the blocks in the desired position – can be overcome quite easily. For more details see the 'Easy access to BlockCAD' file (Item 3.1) on the DVD. We have found it is crucial to link the student teachers' practical experiences of the program to the learning of space and shape in order to avoid BlockCAD merely being seen as a form of 'playing' rather than as a mathematical tool.

Anticipating and analysing pupils' solutions

Linking theory and practice is one of the overall aims and major challenges of teacher preparation programs. In early numeracy, this includes the analysis of pupils' strategies and solutions based on pedagogical content knowledge (Shulman, 1987). The anticipation and analysis of pupils' approaches and procedures with respect to their construction processes appears to be an effective exercise for future teachers, because they learn to identify strategies and link them to developing spatial skills. A suitable task for them, therefore, might be:

A new playground is being built next to our school. This plan shows the unfinished construction of a climbing equipment area. It is a symmetrical design with the line of symmetry right behind the top plate. Can you finish the climbing equipment? (In case you wish to use this task in your class, the BlockCAD file in a LGO-format can be found on the DVD – see Item 3.2.)

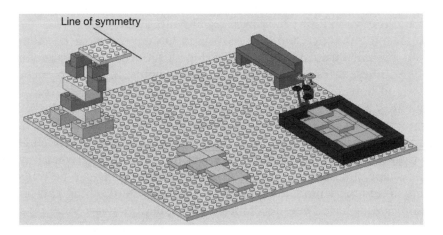

Figure 3.8 *Plan of the playground*

The following text shows what Anna – one of our students – thought might be the potential difficulties and possible pupils' strategies with respect to this task:

This task might present a challenge for some pupils because it is a spatial activity. It may be that the children have only encountered symmetry in class as 2-D learning environments. What makes the task difficult is the fact that the construction has to be mirrored. In order to construct the missing half of the climbing equipment, the pupils have to build from the bottom to the top and cannot continue by adding the second top plate. Less able children might try to build top to bottom – continuing directly with the finished part of the equipment. So the difficulty might be to find a starting point for the construction on the ground. One strategy might be trial and error which could turn out to be time consuming and frustrating. Another (more sophisticated approach) would be to experiment with the blocks in order to find the position of the two parallel ground blocks. Once these two blocks have been positioned, the positions of the other blocks can be found by analysing and comparing their spatial relationships in the given part of the climbing equipment and translating that relationship into a mirror image. I'm assuming that the children would use the block that was positioned last as a reference point. Since it will be difficult (if not impossible) to place all the blocks in the given perspective, children will need to change the views of the object by rotating and tilting it.

When we have asked pre-service teachers to compare their thinking on the demands of the task and pupils' likely approaches and strategies we have found that they are keen to know what really happens in class. We suggest therefore that they are given the opportunity to observe pupils at work and then compare their assumptions with what they saw in the classroom. Another possibility is to use the software 'Camtasia' to demonstrate and analyse pupils' solutions in college (especially when classroom explorations are not possible for organisational reasons). Camtasia is a program that records all computer screen activities and allows them to be played back as a video. It also allows audio recording to include verbal explanations and expressions by the computer user. In the BlockCAD environment you might find this very helpful for accessing and documenting pupils' strategies. We have found such strategies to be an invaluable basis for discussion in teacher education, because the final product – that is, the construction – does not provide sufficient information on the strategies people adopt and the actual construction *process*.

Developing and trialling learning environments

The current lack of BlockCAD related tasks for the primary mathematics classroom presents a great stimulus and motivation for pre-service teachers to develop suitable activities and to trial them when on teaching practice. On our courses in Oldenburg we ask students to do this in groups of five or six individuals. Each group develops a set of tasks that are collected and made into a little booklet. These tasks are then trialled in classrooms. In order to encourage interaction between pupils (and hence make their ideas and thinking explicit), children work in pairs on these tasks while they are observed by a student teacher. The student teachers' detailed notes of the pupils' approaches, strategies and any difficulties they experienced provide authentic data for subsequent seminar discussions and, in some cases, the modification and/or elimination of tasks.

Crucially, we always remind the student teachers to keep in mind what pupils should learn about space and shape and how the specific features of BlockCAD can be utilised to foster and support learning in this curriculum area beyond the traditional teaching and learning materials.

Several examples that have been developed and trialled in classrooms by student teachers will be introduced in the following section. More 'ready to use' tasks and worksheets can be found in the BlockCAD section of the accompanying DVD.

It is important to recognise, however, that not all tasks that can be developed with the focus on mathematics teaching and learning are appropriate for BlockCAD.

Identify the shapes that are nets of a cube. Write the letters F (front), B (back), T (top), G (ground), R (right) and L (left) on the sides.

Figure 3.9 *Nets of a cube*

The solution to the task in Figure 3.9 is clearly not supported by BlockCAD. Children who struggle with the mental folding process in order to check whether the net can be turned into a cube do not benefit from its representation in a Lego context. As the arrangement of the six squares cannot be moved using BlockCAD, the program does not support pupils' developing mental spatial awareness in this instance. Providing paper shapes in this context is far more appropriate because it allows folding activities which help pupils to develop a mental image of the folding process necessary for identifying nets of solid shapes. In other words, BlockCAD in the context of nets of solid shapes is a (superfluous) toy rather than a tool that fosters mathematical understanding (see Buchanan, 2003).

Communicating Activities for the Classroom

When introducing primary pupils to BlockCAD their experiences with computers at home become very obvious. Hence, it is important to assess the children's familiarity with computers thoroughly before using them as tools for learning about space and shape in class. It might be wise to give children the opportunity to work with the computer in other curriculum areas beforehand and to highlight similarities with standard word processing features when introducing it. We were surprised that some individuals felt anxious about using the mouse, because they were afraid of 'doing something wrong'!

Before you start using BlockCAD with your class we strongly recommend that you think through some key questions. For example, to assess whether BlockCAD is a suitable tool for the teaching and learning of a particular mathematical topic you might find it helpful to consider the following questions:

- What other teaching and learning materials might I use in this context?
- Which particular BlockCAD features provide learning and/or visualisation opportunities that other materials do not offer?
- Do the pupils have the required computer skills to enable them to succeed with the task? What type of support might the less computer literate children require?
- What learning processes do I anticipate and to what extent are they supported by BlockCAD?
- What alternatives can I provide for pupils who struggle for different reasons? What might these reasons be?

When the answers to these questions are predominantly positive, we think you'll find that BlockCAD will be a useful – and usually very motivating – tool in the primary mathematics classroom.

The following two BlockCAD tasks illustrate the program's potential for teaching and learning about space and shape. In the first task BlockCAD is used indirectly to create a learning environment and in the second pupils used the program on the computer.

The first task belongs to a unit we created called, 'We help to rebuild the Lego village' (see Items 3.9a–3.9l on the DVD).

Tobias and Jana from the Lego village worked together to build a monument. They built it twice, so that Jana could take her small version of the monument home. But on her way home, she fell off her bicycle. A part of the monument tumbled out and fell into the drain!

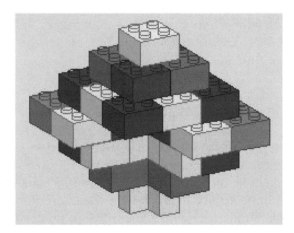

Figure 3.10 *Broken Lego monument*

She was so sad that all of her friends tried rebuilding the lost piece. But which is the correct one for her to use? (See Item 3.9e on the DVD)

Peter (nine-years-old) carefully checked the replacement pieces and argued why they would or would not fit. He marked the wrong block(s) and wrote a comment next to each of the pictures.

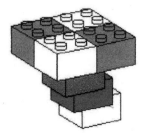

'The white block is too big.'

Figure 3.11a *Replacement piece A*

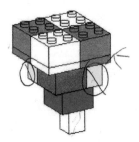

'These blocks are wrong.'
(Peter made a mistake here as only the thin layer is wrong: the two blocks he has circled are correct.)

Figure 3.11b *Replacement piece B*

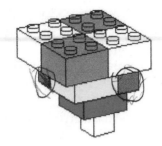

'Colours mixed up.'

Figure 3.11c   Replacement piece C

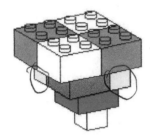

First he wrote that the two blocks he had circled had to be removed. But after checking the next part he changed his mind and crossed out his first comment realising that this was the correct piece.

Figure 3.11d   Replacement piece D

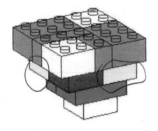

'These are too big.'

Figure 3.11e   Replacement piece E

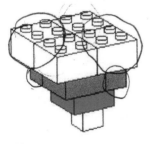

'Wrong colours.'

Figure 3.11f   Replacement piece F

Comparing his solutions with a partner, Peter quickly realised that his comment regarding the second piece was wrong when he compared it with the correct (fourth) piece.

While most pupils in Peter's class could – after some effort and hard thinking – successfully identify the correct piece (either working alone or with a partner), others had great difficulty in finding the solution using only the 2-D representations of the monument and the six pieces. For those children the teacher had prepared real Lego models, so that they could work in a 3-D environment and still link the pieces with their 2-D representations. This way all pupils managed to find the solution and the class could finally attach the missing piece to the monument by using the Lego models. (The LGO-file of the Lego monument can be found on the DVD – see Item 3.3.)

During the whole class discussion two main strategies became obvious. Some children had used their spatial skills to imagine which piece might fit. Others – like Peter – had found the solution by structuring the pieces in terms of colour, block size and shape. The children were surprised to realize that there were two quite different ways of solving the task. Some tried to check whether 'the other way' would also give them the right answer and then pondered on which strategy might be easier for them.

We were pleased that we had asked the children to make a record of their comments so that they could recall their thinking and compare it with other strategies. Interestingly, it turned out that the written comments of the 'structural thinkers' were generally shorter and easier to understand than the ones based on spatial imagery.

We also found BlockCAD to be a great tool for cooperative learning – especially for working in pairs. The pupils discuss their ideas and strategies and have to come to an agreement on what to do and how to share the work, as the following examples from a grade 3 classroom illustrate.

Anne-Marie: *I'll look for the right blocks in the right colours and you put them in the right place, okay? That way we'll both be doing the building.*

Rebecca: *Okay, good idea.*

Julian :   *No, look more carefully: when you turn it [the block] like this, it looks different.*

Tom: *Huh? I don't get it. That way the block is placed completely differently.*

Julian: *Now I am confused. Let's do this part again and then check.*

Tom: *Okay, then you will see that I am right.*

The second task we would like to share with you is based on a Lego construction in the shape of an octahedron (see Figure 3.12) provided by the teacher. (For the LGO-file of the octahedron, see Item 3.4 on the DVD.) This task can require a bit of preparation on your part when planning the lesson to ensure that each pair (or group) of pupils has a Lego object to work with. You could, however, use Lego objects that your pupils have made beforehand if you prefer. The task is as follows:

> Rebuild this shape in BlockCAD. Then make a construction plan that shows how the shape is made, so that other children can also make it.

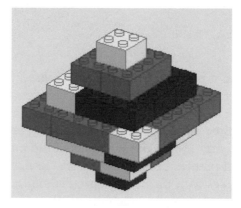

Figure 3.12 *Lego octahedron*

In order to complete this task the pupils need to know what is meant by 'construction plan'. This concept can be introduced either by the genuine construction plans that come with Lego toys or by references to Folding Posters similar to those discussed in Chapter 2. Another option is to introduce construction plans generated using BlockCAD. The construction plan shown in Figure 3.13, for example, shows the building of the octahedron in Figure 3.12. (The Word file of this construction plan can be found on the DVD – see Item 3.5.)

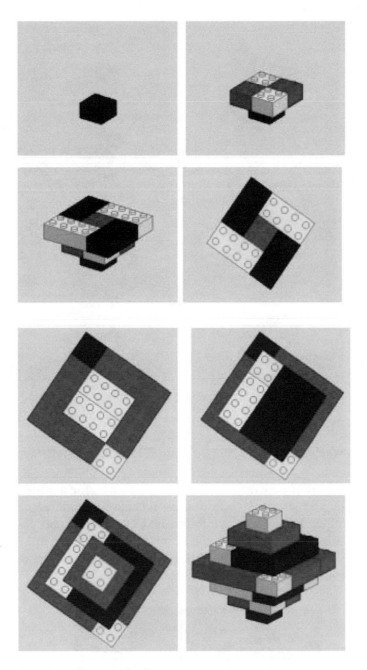

Figure 3.13   *Construction plan octahedron*

While the first task – to rebuild the octahedron in BlockCAD – is fairly easy once you know the program, the second part of the task requires the use of a word processing program such as 'Word' or 'Word Pad'. The children need to know how to make a JPG-file in BlockCAD and how to copy this JPG-file into Word. This sounds more complicated than it really is and we found that in every class we have worked with, there were some children who understood how to do it very quickly and who then showed the others. The procedure is described in detail in the 'Easy Access to BlockCAD' file on the DVD (see Item 3.1). Once the pupils have saved their construction plans as Word or Word Pad files they can be printed on a colour printer and then exchanged with another pair for 'final approval'. Figures 3.14 and 3.15 show two different construction plans designed by year 4 pupils. (For the Word files of the documents see Items 3.6 and 3.7 on the DVD.) While the plan in Figure 3.14 shows the construction from the top to the bottom, the plan in Figure 3.15 suggests building the object from the bottom to the top as in standard constructions in the real world.

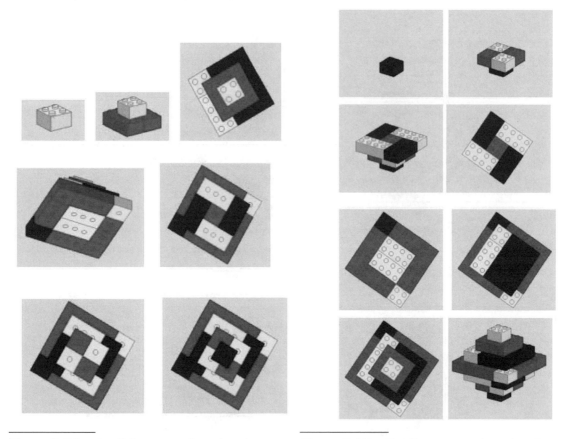

Figure 3.14   *Pupils' construction plan A*   **Figure 3.15**   *Pupils construction plan B*

Again, you can use the different construction plans as the basis for a whole group discussion. Children thoroughly enjoy and learn much from their reflections on different building strategies and their considerations of the best way to communicate the various stages of construction.

In order to cater for mixed ability classes the combination of the virtual construction with real Lego blocks can be a useful support for children who prefer to document their construction in 3-D prior – or parallel – to their virtual construction.

Figure 3.16   *Constructing with Lego blocks*

When comparing the different plans in class, we noted that many pairs tried to show the construction process in as much detail as possible. However, having used the plans for reconstruction, the children concluded that the most detailed plans were not necessarily the best ones; indeed they discovered that essential information about the construction process could often be communicated effectively in shorter plans with fewer pictures. Children who have finished the task quickly can thus be challenged by giving them variations of the task format and asking them to condense the plans. When Bernd Wollring, a colleague from the University of Kassel and COSIMA partner, trialled this task with student teachers in a local primary school they developed the following task variations:

- The construction plan has to fit onto one A4 page.
- The construction plan can have no more than seven (or even no more than five) pictures.
- Make a construction plan for a kindergarten child.

These plans can then be used to stimulate classroom discussion focusing on what information is essential and what is superfluous for creating an effective reconstruction.

Figure 3.17 shows a plan with only five pictures. When criticised by peers that the top block is missing, its developers, Karen and Jade, argued that you would know what the top block looked like from the picture. They then admitted that it would be better to add the block in the plan (Item 3.8 on the DVD provides the Word file of this plan).

Figure 3.17 *Plan using five pictures only*

A pair of year 4 pupils who developed a plan for kindergarten children (see Figure 3.18) decided to include the number of the blocks in each layer 'in order to help the children to count'.

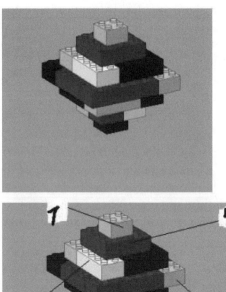

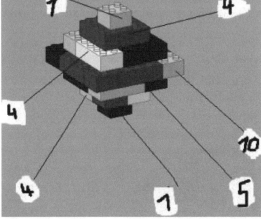

Figure 3.18   *Plan for kindergarten children*

Once pupils are familiar with BlockCAD we found it a great environment for individual learning as well. Being installed and available on one (or more) computer(s) in the class, individual children can work on a variety of tasks of varying degrees of difficulty during periods when they can decide what they want to work on. On the DVD you can find a whole collection of tasks related to the Lego village (see Items 3.9a–3.9l) designed for this purpose (these can also can be used with everyone during a lesson). A sheet with the task overview (Item 3.9c) helps the pupils to keep track of what tasks they have already completed.

Last, but not least, we found that many pupils reacted enthusiastically when we invited them to develop BlockCAD-based tasks themselves – either for their own classmates or children in other classes in the school. Many found it especially appealing to devise tasks for younger children who had very particular needs (see above).

Communicating Ideas for In-service Courses

A good starting point for in-service sessions might be to get the teachers to reflect on their teaching about space and shape: are they confident that their classroom activities cover the National Numeracy Strategy? What works well for them? What are pupils' common mistakes? What do they think their pupils learn with respect to space and shape? What out-of-school experiences do the children bring to school? What materials do they use for visualisation? Do they use ICT for teaching space and shape and/or in other areas of early numeracy? What are their experiences? What would they like to change in order to improve teaching and learning?

A discussion of shared and individual experiences and approaches can then form the basis for an introduction to BlockCAD. We found that it works well to use pupils' examples to illustrate BlockCAD's potential for the connection of modern approaches to the teaching and learning of space and shape which advocate the use of ICT in all curriculum areas. A construction plan generated by pupils (for example, see Figures 3.13, 3.14, 3.15 or 3.17) might be the starting point for teachers' exploration of the program and its specific features. Furthermore the comparison and analysis of different plans will provide insight into pupils' building strategies.

It is important that teachers become familiar with the program and get involved in BlockCAD related tasks themselves prior to classroom implementation. In so doing they begin to anticipate the problems that pupils might encounter and to plan their lessons accordingly. The introduction and exploration of the program's specific features, however, can be combined with the planning of classroom materials. Figure 3.19 shows the preparation of a group of Czech teachers from the COSIMA project for a classroom experiment and Figure 3.20 shows one pupil's solution to the first task.

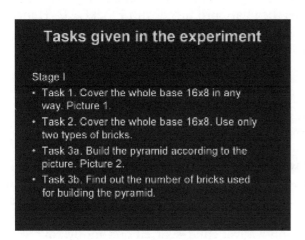

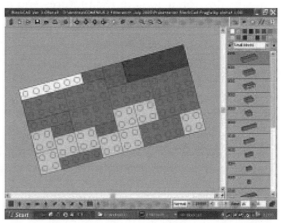

Figure 3.19   *Tasks by Czech teachers*   **Figure 3.20**   *Pupil's solution to task 1*

If the aim of a lesson is to discover levels of symmetry, the goal of an activity for in-service teachers might be to develop appropriate objects for the classroom.

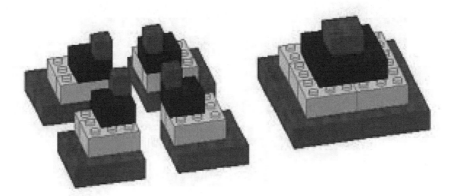

Figure 3.21   *Lines of symmetry in a Block CAD pyramid*

The example shown in Figure 3.21 by two German teachers involves the idea of the group concept (see section 'Communicating the Theme'): that only one of four segments has to be constructed before it is copied and rotated in order to construct a pyramid.

As highlighted in the section 'Communicating Activities for the Classroom' we feel it is important to encourage teachers to develop tasks that are suitable for pupils with mixed abilities. In our experience the combination of BlockCAD with real Lego blocks is usually a great support for learners whose spatial skills are slower to develop than their classmates. Furthermore, in one of our classroom explorations, all the children eagerly compared real and virtual building strategies with respect to their specific possibilities on the one hand and their restrictions on the other hand.

Communicating Related Follow-up Activities

The related follow-up activities we would like to suggest are cross-curricular use and 'maths pen pals'.

BlockCAD is not only an effective tool in early numeracy: it can also be used in other curriculum areas once the children are familiar with it. In our experience children are impressed by the 'professional' look of the pictures and plans they have produced with BlockCAD. Hence, you might consider BlockCAD

- to illustrate the children's creative writing;
- to build a medieval village;
- to make a 3-D plan of the school;
- to use for art projects.

In order to stress its communicative opportunities, why not use BlockCAD in a 'pen pal' project with another school? Communication and correspondence with friends and peers abroad (or in the neighbouring school) is frequently limited to written texts and hand-drawn pictures. Using BlockCAD to communicate construction plans of Lego objects created by pupils helps to highlight mathematical communication in an innovative, child-centred and motivating way. In particular, children with restricted language abilities, or with English as an Additional Language, are not limited by their verbal/writing skills when communicating with partners 1000 m or 1000 km away. The fact that BlockCAD files in the LGO-format are very small, makes it easy to send them and/or related Word documents as attachments via email.

Summary of Key Ideas

- BlockCAD helps to link school mathematics learning with children's out-of-school experiences (and competencies).
- BlockCAD is a useful tool for helping pupils relate 3-D objects/models to their 2-D representations.
- BlockCAD connects the teaching and learning of space and shape with the use of ICT and supports 'computer literacy'.
- BlockCAD fosters alternative forms of mathematical communication in the classroom and beyond.
- BlockCAD helps to link early numeracy with other subjects.

Pause for Reflection

- When you think about your teaching with respect to space and shape, what do children tend to struggle with, what are the common mistakes?
- In numeracy sessions how do you cater for learners with restricted verbal communication skills such as those with a non-English speaking background?
- What classroom materials do you usually use when teaching space and shape? How do they compare to BlockCAD?
- What would you stress if you wanted to convince a colleague to use BlockCAD in class?

Further Reading

Haylock, D. (2005) *Mathematics Explained for Primary Teachers*. London: Sage Publications
In Chapters 24 (Transformations and Symmetry) and 25 (Classifying Shapes) Derek Haylock discusses key concepts in primary school geometry in a very accessible and informative way.

Johnston-Wilder S. and Mason J. (2005) *Developing Thinking in Geometry*. London: Paul Chapman Publishing
This is an informative book which integrates subject knowledge and pedagogy through a variety of tasks, including interactive activities on a CD. The writers encourage the reader to think more deeply about teaching and learning and the nature of shape and space.

Way, J. and Beardon, T. (eds) (2003) *ICT and Primary Mathematics*. Maidenhead: Open University Press.
While this book does not explicitly make connections to BlockCAD, we enjoyed reading about different ways of using ICT in primary mathematics in order to promote mathematics teaching and learning. The key idea is to use ICT deliberately and as 'tools not toys' in class. The examples given in the book by experienced and enthusiastic teachers and teacher educators strongly support this approach.

References

Buchanan, M. (2003) Classroom technologies as tools not toys: a teacher's perspective on making it work in the classroom. In J. Way and T. Beardon (eds), *ICT and Primary Mathematics* (pp. 122–152). Maidenhead: Open University Press.

Lewis, H. (1963) Spatial representation in drawing as a correlate of development and a basis for picture reference, *Journal of Genetic Psychology 102*, 95–107.

Shulman, L. (1987) Knowledge and teaching: Foundations of a new reform, *Harvard Educational Review 57*, 1–22.

Exploring Movement through ICT

Fiona Thangata and Alan Pagden

Communicating the Theme

Two pupils, Alex and Emily, entered the following instructions into a floor robot – PIP:

  CM, F 50, P 20, B 50 GO (CM = clear memory, F = forward, P = pause, B = back)

They watched PIP's movement and then each predicted what the graph of the movement would look like when PIP was set to move in front of a distance sensor (Ranger). Here are their predictions:

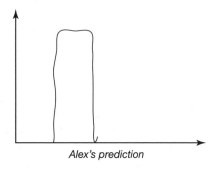

Alex's prediction

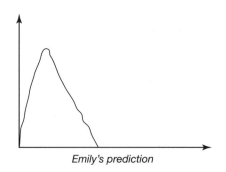

Emily's prediction

Imagine their surprise when PIP's movements generated the following line graph on the computer screen:

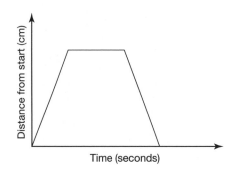

'You got it wrong,' said Alex, 'you missed out the pause.'

'You got it wrong as well,' replied Emily.

'No I didn't,' said Alex, pointing to the horizontal line on his graph, 'this is what happens when PIP is waiting.'

'Yes but look,' insisted Emily, 'you started in the wrong place.'

The example above may appear to involve mathematical ideas often only found in the later primary years and beyond. As we will demonstrate, however, an early introduction to movement, time and space provides opportunities for young children to gain an intuitive understanding of distance–time graphs and angles in a child-centred and interesting way. Our aim is to make their first experiences of these complex topics both positive and meaningful, thus reducing the likelihood of anxiety and incomprehension when they later encounter a more formal and abstract approach.

In this chapter we describe how to combine activities in primary mathematics that exploit two different information technology devices. The first involves the use of floor robots (i.e. programmable toys) first discussed by Papert in 1980. The second device involves the use of data-logging equipment. These are sensors that gather information from the environment and use computer software to process it. Although it is more often found in a science context (see, for example, Roger Frost's website: www.rogerfrost.com), we have found it to be a very effective teaching tool in primary mathematics. There are now many different data-logging devices available and a wide range of sensors suitable for use in primary schools. The particular set of data-logging equipment used in the COSIMA project included the Ranger distance sensor with LogIT software, which is described below. Whilst the use of floor robots and data loggers are established practices in many primary classrooms in England (for example, they are prescribed in the primary National Curriculum), their combination in this working environment is novel and, we believe, both exciting and full of potential.

Many of you will be familiar with the use of a floor turtle (Roamer, PIP, Pixie and so on) and may wish to skip this section, but its key features are outlined below for those who are not familiar with how it works.

Several programmable floor devices are available for the primary classroom. PIP (www. swallow.co.uk) and Roamer (www.valiant-technology.com) are among the best known in the UK and have been around for over 20 years. Interestingly PIP is an acronym for 'programmable interactive plaything', reflecting its designer's vision of learning through play (Papert, 1980). PIP (and its newer version PIPPIN) is a cuboid-shaped robot on wheels whose movements are measured in centimetres and which turns in degrees, although it can also be configured to move in larger units (steps of 10 degrees and/or 10cm) (Figure 4.1).

Figure 4.1 PIP floor robot

When working with PIP for the first time it is important to be aware of one of its foibles: it remembers the last program that was entered and so new programs need to start with CM (clear memory). If you forget to do this you may be puzzled by its actions only to discover it was moving as its previous operator instructed! Pressing CM is a routine that children readily adopt. To programme PIP you then choose from the control panel a command key to say what PIP should do (for example, move Forward or Back, turn Left or Right) followed by one or more number keys to specify how much it should move or turn. The effect of single commands (such as forward 20) can be seen, or a sequence of instructions can be programmed, before instructing PIP to move. We often place a marker pen through the hole in the centre of PIP so that we can all watch as its path is reproduced on paper. This serves as a record of the movement and is very useful as a focus for discussion and analysis. One very powerful command is the Repeat button (RPT), which allows you to tell PIP how many times you want it to repeat an instruction or set of instructions. You will find examples later in the chapter of the fun children had with this.

The other main device used is the LogIT Ranger (www.dcpmicro.com/), one of many sensors that are available to operate with a 'data logger' and appropriate software (Figure 4.2). Most data loggers can be used independently of a computer but we have found it most effective if children observe the results 'live' on a computer screen. The Ranger records the distance, or 'displacement' of an object or person from the sensor. The ultrasonic beam that is emitted bounces back to the Ranger from the first object – say a person – it encounters, continuously measuring the distance between the two while the latter – in this case the person – moves. Linked to a computer and used with LogIT software (one of several packages available) the Ranger produces distance–time graphs from the displacement (movement) data in real time. Children are able to watch the movement of a person or a floor turtle and the resulting graph as it emerges on the screen simultaneously. In a whole class teaching context the Ranger set-up needs to be connected to a screen that is as large as possible (Figure 4.3). As you will soon realise, the Ranger can only sense an object at a distance of between 20cm and 300cm, so PIP has to stay within this range in order to keep its movements visible on the graph.

Figure 4.2 *Ranger distance sensor*

The teachers in the COSIMA countries used the equipment in a variety of ways and, as you will discover through the activities we discuss, are focused less on learning about technology (although this is a natural consequence) and more on using technology to develop a greater understanding of mathematical ideas and concepts.

Figure 4.3   *Children walking in front of Ranger to produce distance–time graphs*

Communicating the Concepts

One of the most powerful aspects of this learning environment is that children can lead their own learning. Indeed, Siraj-Blatchford and Whitebread (2003) noted that children gain knowledge most effectively when they are in control of their own learning and are encouraged to be playful. Interestingly, as early as 1654, the Czech writer Comenius wrote about the benefits of play in learning, in *School as Play* (*Schola Ludus*). The use of a programmable 'toy' alone, or together with the ranger, allows children to set their own goals and ask 'what if we try this?' questions. We have observed that they quickly become involved in communication with the floor robot and with each other as they plan what to do, watch the effect of their instructions and refine their programs in the light of the feedback given by PIP's movements and/or the graphs produced.

When children play with PIP and/or Ranger they encounter a range of communication strategies. For example, PIP responds to its instructions by movement. It understands certain forms of language and children adapt to the particular style needed to make it move in the way they want it to. Thus, when using PIP children are translating between various forms of communication: for example, what they want PIP to do, the set of instructions they type in, the visible movement of PIP and the trace it leaves on paper if a pen is attached. When using Ranger, we have observed children translating between their own movement in front of the distance sensor and the distance–time graph produced. To interpret the distance–time graph, they need to consider both time and distance and relate how they moved to a two-dimensional representation – the graph – of their movement. When the two devices, PIP and Ranger, are used together, children begin to understand the relationship between the instructions they feed into PIP and the graph produced by its movement. Matching the shape of a graph with a sequence of movements witnessed first hand represents a significant achievement on the part of the child who has to coordinate two very different things in their head simultaneously.

Our teachers frequently found that if children are asked to interpret distance–time graphs produced by the Ranger they often reveal certain misconceptions. For example, a horizontal line in the graph is read as a movement of the object to the right when in fact it represents a pause (see the dialogue between Alex and Emily which began this chapter). If, however, you ask a child to be the 'object' in front of the Ranger then they begin to notice that if they stand still a horizontal line on a distance–time graph will result. By making this discovery the child begins to understand how the dimension of time is represented in the graph. As you will discover, other misconceptions about graphs frequently emerge. Through this process of challenging and interesting mathematical 'play' children are given access to difficult concepts at an earlier age than through traditional methods which rely on paper and pencil methods and the interpretation of abstract – and often, in pupils' eyes, meaningless – graphs.

Our project teachers usually introduced PIP by getting children to act out 'robot' movements with their own bodies, for example the children follow similar instructions to those that are executed by the robot, PIP. This helps the children interpret commands from PIP's point of view. Once this has been achieved they begin to appreciate how, for example, the relationship between a square PIP has drawn and the movements that it made to draw that square. Here only one variable – movement – is considered.

When you begin to work with both PIP and the Ranger children need to focus on two different variables – distance and time. You might think that this would be more difficult for them, however we have not found this to be the case as pupils are usually highly intrigued by the activities we set.

Communicating Experiences with Pre-service Teachers

The learning environment consists of three parts, corresponding to the technological devices used: PIP alone, Ranger alone and Ranger in conjunction with PIP. These are described below in terms of the stages that the pre-service teachers in the UK, Germany and the Czech Republic worked through with them.

PIP

PIP was used in a variety of different ways in the COSIMA countries. When it is first introduced, many pre-service teachers think it is no more than a fun 'toy' to play with (Hunscheidt and Peter-Koop, 2006). Floor robots certainly are fun to play with, and through playing with PIP there is a lot of mathematics that children can learn. We will now describe how the pre-service teachers have been challenged to develop mathematically meaningful learning environments using PIP.

The pre-service teachers first became familiar with the keypad on PIP and all the functions available. They explored how to program PIP to move, including the use of the Repeat (RPT) key and turning PIP through different angles. A popular activity with the pre-service teachers in the UK was to set up an obstacle course and plan how to move PIP around it, without crashing into any of the obstacles! Another idea was to program PIP to move through a maze. Student teachers felt that these would provide worthwhile, and enjoyable, learning opportunities for children. Other successful activities included programming PIP to move around a street plan, a river, or model of another 'real life' environment, which offered opportunities for cross-curricular and topic work. PIP can be 'dressed up' as a vehicle, person or character (Figure 4.4).

Figure 4.4 *PIP as a truck*

The student teachers also explored how to instruct PIP to draw a variety of polygons. A common starting point was to draw a square. If you want PIP to move in a square, or draw a square on paper, try pressing the following commands:

CM

Forward 50 Right 90

Forward 50 Right 90

Forward 50 Right 90

Forward 50 Right 90

Go

As you can appreciate, if we wanted to draw a 20-sided polygon (an icosagon) this would involve a lot of repetitious programming! This is where the Repeat command comes in handy. A shorter program for drawing a square is:

CM Repeat 4 [Forward 50 Right 90] GO

Interestingly, when the pre-service teachers tried to draw an equilateral triangle, many of them chose an angle of 60° for PIP to turn through. Can you work out why this did not produce a triangle? With the pre-service teachers, as with children, we found that a useful hint was to encourage them to stand up and walk the shape themselves, thinking about the turns they were making. This led them to the realisation that when you 'walk' a polygon, the angle you turn at each vertex is the exterior angle rather than the interior angle! When you walk around the whole shape you turn through 360°, leading to the understanding that each exterior angle of a regular polygon is equal to 360° divided by the number of angles in the polygon. So, to draw an equilateral triangle you would choose an angle of 120° rather than 60°. Try writing a program to draw a regular pentagon.

This strategy of walking the shape also came in handy when thinking about how to program PIP to move in a circle. Initially, the pre-service teachers were puzzled by this as PIP moves in straight lines, not curves! By walking a circle, and describing their movement, they figured out how to program PIP. As one said; ' I am taking lots of tiny steps, and turning a little bit each time'.

From these explorations the students developed an understanding of the mathematical potential of using PIP in a classroom setting. The next stage was to plan how to introduce PIP to primary children. Some of the pre-service teachers in Germany, for example, created a large chart of some of PIP's keys (Figure 4.5) as a way of introducing children to the main features. The pre-service teachers found that it was necessary to explain to the children that each time you program PIP you first need to press CM (clear memory) so that it does not repeat commands stored previously. It can be quite puzzling when you have put in your commands and pressed GO to see PIP making different movements than the ones you programmed!

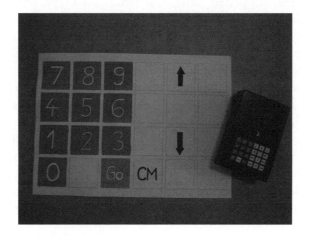

Figure 4.5   *Chart to show key functions on PIP*

Some pre-service teachers chose to focus on introducing children to angles through the use of PIP. Geometry and angle-drawing computer programs are also available to give children a more dynamic view of angle as a measure of turn. What PIP offers is 'the introduction of angle in a hands-on and discovery based environment that involves and challenges the exploration of a number of angles other than 90° and their relationships' (Hunscheidt and Peter-Koop, 2006). The pre-service teachers in Germany and the Czech Republic developed a learning environment to introduce students to 90°, 180° and 360° as a way of finding and estimating angles in between these values. A diagram of a circle was prepared on a large piece of paper, with the centre marked and radii at 10° intervals drawn on it (Figure 4.6). An arrow was attached to the front of PIP to show the angle it turned through. The teachers prepared various tasks and challenges for the children (see section on activities for the classroom below).

Figure 4.6   *Using PIP to learn about angles*

Ranger

Before using Ranger in the classroom, the pre-service teachers needed time to explore how to set it up, how it works and investigate its limitations. For example, they discovered that the person or object moving in front of the sensor needs to stay in line with the Ranger because if you move to the left or right you are likely to go outside the narrow beam and not be detected. Also, the readings are not reliable if the person or object is very close (nearer than 20cm) to the Ranger or too far away (over 3m). This is useful for the pre-service teachers to know so that they can help the children interpret the graphs produced when using the Ranger. Several teachers remarked on the importance of spending time trying out the Ranger before using it in the classroom. Familiarity with the equipment gave the teachers confidence in the classroom, especially when the 'unexpected' happened. Several teachers also remarked how they learned along with the children and how this provided a good model for the children.

The pre-service teachers used the Ranger to produce and interpret graphs of their own movement in front of the sensor. Since the Ranger was new to them, they were put in the position of being learners. Many were keen to try out their own ideas – 'What if we walked like this?', 'How could we make a graph like this?', 'Is it possible to make a circle?', 'Is it possible to make any capital letter shapes?' Through this exploration, the pre-service teachers learned more about the Ranger and its possibilities in the classroom. They discovered what would be interesting and challenging activities for children to try. One example from Milan in the Czech Republic was about creating a discontinuous graph (Figure 4.8). When he asked the student teachers if it was possible to create such a graph using Ranger, several teachers tried to cover the computer screen before realising that they could create a discontinuous graph with their own movement. You might like to pause for a moment and consider how this might be done.

Figure 4.7   *Using Range in the classroom in Germany*

Figure 4.8   *Discontinuous graph*

One method that worked was for a teacher to step in and out of the Ranger's beam. Another group came up with the idea of having several people standing in a line, taking turns to jump in and out of the beam at different distances from the Ranger. The pre-service teachers were excited by the many possibilities for children to explore their own ideas.

PIP plus Ranger

The pre-service teachers also explored the use of PIP in conjunction with Ranger. As above, they needed to spend time becoming familiar with setting up the equipment.

Figure 4.9   *Exploring with PIP and Ranger*

A good starting point is to explore how the graphs made by PIP differ from those made by a person moving in front of the Ranger. Since PIP always moves at the same speed, the graphs will consist of straight lines only and the lines will all have the same slope. This makes it easier to repeat movements or to make, for example, a symmetrical graph. The student teachers observed that it was qualitatively different to program PIP to move than watch a person moving. The lines of communication are different since one has to program PIP before it will move. Connections can be made between the sequence of instructions given to PIP, PIP's movement, and the graph produced. Given any one of these, it is possible to work out the other two. In this way, student teachers (and pupils) can make sense of the linked, multiple representations: written program, physical movement, graph.

Classroom organisation

One focus for discussion was about managing the classroom environment. Most of the student teachers felt that they would be more confident to use PIP with a group of children first of all, rather than the whole class. With Ranger it was slightly different, since if you can show the graphs on a projector screen the whole class can be involved in the discussion. The student teachers also expressed the need to be very familiar with how to set up the equipment, how it works, and what to do if it doesn't work properly. 'I would be a bit nervous in case I broke PIP or the Ranger', said one student teacher. Others were more confident and remarked how the children often pick up how to use new technology faster than the teacher!

Communicating Activities for the Classroom

PIP

Children's first introduction to PIP is often to become familiar with the different buttons. They like to explore what happens when you program it to move Forward 10, Back 20, and so on. Through the use of a large format diagram of some of PIP's buttons children can find out for themselves what each button is for. Another starting activity is to program PIP to move in front of the children and then ask them to recall what PIP did. In this way they can begin to link the sequence of commands with actions.

Young children can sit in a circle and program PIP to move from a starting point to another person, estimating the distance to be travelled (Figure 4.10). Through the use of cards showing the different buttons, children begin to build up a sequence of moves, and make these sequences into a program. Immediate feedback is provided once PIP is set off to move along the programmed journey. Mistakes or unintentional actions are evident and the children can discuss and refine their program. The children can also move around the learning environment, interacting with PIP and exploring their world.

Figure 4.10   *Exploring with PIP*

In some classrooms, children recorded their sequence of instructions and wrote about their experiences of using PIP. In the example shown (Figures 4.11a and 4.11b), the child states the need to press Clear Memory (CM) at the start, to clear the previous instructions from PIP. After the program is entered, Go must be pressed for PIP to start its journey. This early work need not involve the use of angles.

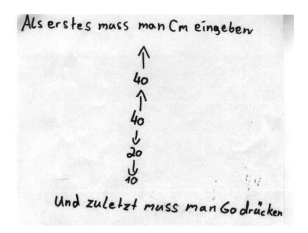

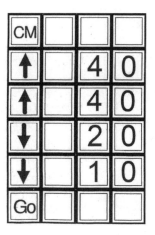

Figure 4.11a *Recording a sequence of instructions for PIP*

Figure 4.11b *The corresponding program for PIP*

As a progression, children can work out how to navigate along a route. At this stage, right angles can be introduced. A left or right turn of 90° offers scope for movement around, for example, a street scene or maze. As children plan their sequence of instructions they have to visualise the journey from the point of view of PIP in order to decide in which direction to turn. This might involve colleagues following behind PIP. Children may experiment with other angles for themselves to see the effect of different amounts of turn. Small group collaboration and discussion is encouraged and these activities are better performed with small groups rather than as a whole class activity (Video clip Item 4.1 on the DVD shows children programming PIP to follow a line.)

Creating a meaningful context, such as visiting places along a street scene, and being able to personalise PIP – by making a cover in the shape of a car, boat, monster for example – adds to the children's interest and motivation, as illustrated by the school bus scene in Figures 4.12a and 4.12b. (Video clip Item 4.2 on the DVD shows the bus making its journey around the town.)

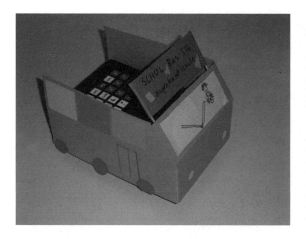

Figure 4.12a *PIP as a school bus in Germany* **Figure 4.12b** *The school bus route*

A teacher in the UK, Audrey, observed that children found it easier to conceptualise time, distance and direction in a story environment. Cross-curricular work was possible, such as this example related to a topic on rivers. The context was of a boat travelling along a stretch of river, stopping at different points to monitor bird life. PIP was 'dressed' as a boat and programmed to travel along the river (Figure 4.13). In another example, a boat sailed from a harbour, visiting islands to set down and pick up passengers. The children can also add or make artefacts to embellish the scene. Other examples included work in Geography looking at distances between countries (Figure 4.14).

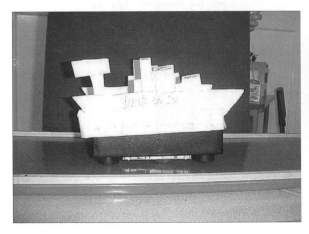

Figure 4.13   *A boat journey with PIP*   **Figure 4.14**   *Using PIP in Geography*

Children in England also wrote stories and sketched graphs to go with situations where there could be movement in a straight line. Figure 4.15, for example, is one girl's story about a bicycle ride. Further examples for stories can be found on the DVD (Item 4.3 'Ideas for movement in a straight line' and Item 4.4 'Storyline table').

A girl on a bike pulling wheelies:
Girl goes forward 5 metres, pulls a wheelie, continues to go forward another 4 metres, pulls another wheelie, completes this facing the way she has come from. Goes forward 8 metres, pulls another wheelie, turns continues for 6 metres, pulls two wheelies, ends facing the other way, goes forward 4 metres and stops.

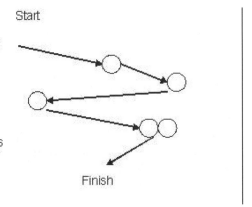

Figure 4.15   *Story contexts*

Using PIP to explore angle

One of the Czech pre-service teachers, Eva, used PIP to teach angles. The children already knew about right angles. Eva drew a circle divided into four quarters on the whiteboard and explained that a right angle is 90°, and showed the children 180°, 270°, and 360° on the diagram. The children placed PIP on a large poster with a circular scale (Figure 4.16). Placing PIP at the centre of the circle facing 0°/360°, the children were asked to explore the effect of programming PIP so it turned 90°, 40°, 180° and so on, in both clockwise and anticlockwise directions. The children were then set challenges such as:

- If PIP is pointing towards 40°, where will it point if it turns 60° anticlockwise.
- If the degrees of the circle are hidden, estimate where PIP will stop if we program it to turn 45°, 120°, etc.

Figure 4.16 *Using PIP to explore angular measure*

In this exploratory, hands-on environment, the children learned about angles earlier than suggested in the curriculum.

The children also used PIP to practise fractions. Again using the circular poster, with PIP placed at the centre, the children were asked to program PIP to divide the circle into sixths (and other fractions). This time, a pen was attached so that PIP's movements left a trace on the paper. This involved the children in much discussion on the use of the angles, PIP's Repeat function, and calculation of fractions of a circle.

Another activity for slightly older children was aimed at understanding the concepts of parallel and perpendicular lines. From a given starting angle, students traced a line that formed the diameter of the circle and were then invited to draw a perpendicular line through the centre of the circle. Another challenge was to draw a line parallel to the original diameter. The idea of parallel and perpendicular lines was introduced to these primary children at an earlier stage than in the regular school mathematics curriculum as they were able to find out about things for themselves, demonstrating a conceptual understanding of angles.

To summarise: such tasks require reasoning and planning. Mistakes are clearly visible and can be rectified through trial and improvement. Students develop their understanding of angle and improve their estimation skills in the light of their experiences with PIP. It encourages experimentation, reflection and visualisation. Some curriculum topics can be introduced earlier than would usually be the case.

Ranger

The Ranger motion sensor, attached to a computer with the LogIT software, was introduced to the children. Many of the children in the classrooms involved in the project were aged between seven and ten-years-old, but these materials can also be used with younger children, although of course the level of interpretation and discussion will vary accordingly. The initial tasks in this learning environment involve a person moving in front of the Ranger and everyone observing the emerging distance–time graph. A range of activities was found to be successful and a suggested progression of stages is discussed below.

Initially, after explaining that you need to keep in front of the Ranger for it to detect you, children can be asked to move in any way they like in front of it. The children might observe the graph that is produced simultaneously with the movement (real time graphing) and think about what is being measured and how.

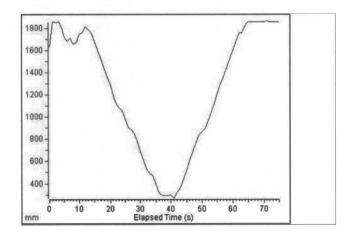

Figure 4.17   *Distance–time graph*

Children can then explore the effect of changing direction and changing speed by analysing the graph. Young children are generally very keen to try out different movements, even acrobatics, in front of the Ranger to see the effect. They can be imaginative and ask 'What would happen if …?' For example, one girl performed a cartwheel to see what the graph would look like. Often someone will suggest having more than one person in front of the Ranger, moving in different ways, to investigate the graphs produced. A typical question from children is 'Can the Ranger pick up more than one person at a time?' This can be tested out by the children, who discover that it is always the nearest person (or object) that is detected. Another question children often ask is 'Can the Ranger work in the dark?'. What do you think? Well, yes, it can!

Children can sketch other graphs that could be produced by the equipment, and then test these out by performing the movements that they predict will generate the graph drawn. The unexpected leads to discussion and helps children understand more about the way the graphs are produced, and the relationship between the two variables of distance and time.

Children can find out whether or not a graph is possible. A tried and tested way into this is to suggest producing a capital letter, such as M. Once children have worked out what movements are needed to produce M, you can pose the question 'What other capital letters can we do?'. The possibility of producing the letter O always leads to interesting discussion. You may immediately realise that it is not possible to create an O, since it would not be the graph of a function. The student teachers found that, initially, in every class where this was discussed, some children were convinced that it would be possible. Typically, some children try walking in a circle (an example of iconic representation, linking the actual path of the movement with the graph) and are surprised by the resulting graph. On seeing two semicircles, other children often suggest having two people in front of the Ranger with each one walking in a semicircle. After many efforts, children conclude for themselves that it will not be possible to draw an O. They are able to give reasons such as, 'You cannot be in two places at one time' or 'The Ranger cannot detect two people at the same time'. Another discussion arises from the challenge to draw the letter N. Many children think this will be possible and devise many strategies to create the vertical line such as running very fast, or having several people stand in front of the Ranger in a line. With experience children conclude that such vertical lines are not possible either because you cannot be detected in more than one place at one time, or it is impossible to move a distance in zero time. These discussions lead to an intuitive understanding of functions, which will be developed in later years.

Children can also interpret written descriptions by drawing graphs, and predicting what graph will be produced by a sequence of moves. They can then check the results. Or they might move in front of the Ranger to overlay a graph produced by their peers and discuss how the speed and direction of the two 'journeys' were similar and how they differed.

Children also enjoy sketching graphs based on the observed movement of a partner, with the screen hidden from view and then comparing their predictions with the computer generated graphs. Another successful activity is to ask them to interpret graphs by writing stories.

Throughout this process many children exhibit common misconceptions. For example, when trying to overlay the graph of a peer, children often move in the wrong direction. Or, when sketching possible alternatives, they frequently construct graphs that go back in time. As mentioned above, in attempting to produce a circle on the computer screen children invariably walk in a circle and are surprised when the graph appears as two arches next to one another. These misconceptions are important indications of the strategies the children are using. The advantage of the Ranger is that there is immediate feedback and children can try again at once, reflecting on why their movement did not produce the expected graph, or why a particular graph is impossible. Children relate the two variables, distance and time, through their own body movements. The steepness of the line represents the speed and, although not formally introduced, children are often able to talk about this aspect after using Ranger.

It is worth noting that although the axes have visible scales (time in seconds, distance in centimetres), there is no need to place much emphasis on these numbers in the initial stages. Children look at the graph as a whole, and what different sections of the graph represent, rather than at specific coordinate points on the graph. More important aspects are the ability to interpret a distance–time graph and develop a greater understanding of the distance–time relationship.

Ranger with PIP

As an alternative to using Ranger with the children moving in front of it, it can be used in conjunction with PIP. A floor robot was chosen because it moves with uniform speed and, therefore, its journeys can be more easily repeated than a person's movements in front of the Ranger.

PIP is placed in front of the Ranger and programmed to move backwards and forwards in a straight line. The main reason for doing this was to provide children with the opportunity to compare and match the line graphs created by the Ranger with the lists of instructions, or programs, given to PIP. Graphs made by PIP are noticeably different from those made by a person. PIP moves at a constant speed and therefore produces graphs that consist only of straight line slopes. There is still plenty of scope for exploration without the added complexity of variable speed.

Typically children are introduced to this learning environment through the following stages:

- Instruct PIP to move to and fro in front of the Ranger and observe the graphs produced.
- Input a sequence of moves and predict what the graph will look like before setting PIP off (or you can hide the computer screen and reveal the graph once everyone has made their predictions).
- Write instructions for PIP to produce graphs that are given (the overlay feature is useful here for testing out the instructions and comparing different graphs).
- Explore ways of representing PIP's movements using numerical statements.
- Record PIP's movements.

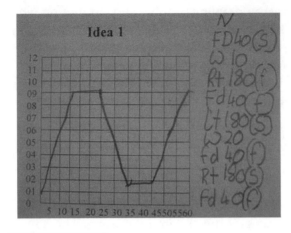

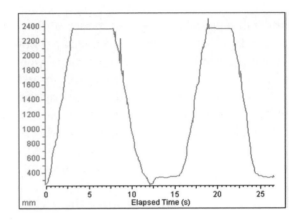

Figure 4.18a   *Predicted graph*   **Figure 4.18b**   *Actual graph*

The classroom activities provide powerful learning opportunities for children to extend their understanding. Children can communicate in various ways: orally, through their discussions in groups or in whole class situations; visually, through predicting and sketching graphs; kinaesthetically, through their own body movements in front of the Ranger; and through the programmed movements of PIP. Children can also explain their reasoning, orally or in written form, reflect on what happened and describe their strategies for solving a problem. All these ways of communicating enhance the likelihood of developing a shared understanding of the relationships between the movements, the programmed instructions and the graphs.

Communicating Ideas for In-service Courses

The activities that have been tried with teachers are the same that the children experience when using PIP and Ranger. In addition, the teachers – like the pre-service teachers – all expressed the importance of knowing how to set up the equipment, how to link the Ranger to the computer, and how to deal with the unexpected! The teachers all felt they would need to spend some time using the equipment, without the children, before introducing it in the classroom. In the same way as the pre-service teachers, through their own exploration of the technology, the teachers became more confident in using it and more aware of its benefits for the classroom. Their own experiences developed their understanding of the concepts involved and led them to view PIP and Ranger as meaningful tools for learning.

Teachers also become aware that the technology does not replace the teacher. As Vincent (2003) states, the teacher is the one who still provides the goal and sets the challenges, but the children can take those challenges further and set new ones, supported by the teacher. Letting-go in this way – although it requires courage on the part of the teacher – allows the children to construct their own meanings and reduces the amount of talk and direct instruction by the teacher. Children with different learning styles are catered for, especially those who prefer to learn in more kinaesthetic and visual ways. Children learning mathematics in a language that is not their first are not as dependent on understanding the teacher's talk, but can extend their learning through being actively involved and watching others.

Communicating Related Follow-up Activities

PIP introduces children to the LOGO programming language. A natural extension to programming a floor robot is to use the computer and LOGO to write programs for on-screen designs. Using the same basic commands, children can build increasingly complex programs (see for example, Papert, 1980). The example in Figure 4.19 is made from squares, rotated to produce an attractive design.

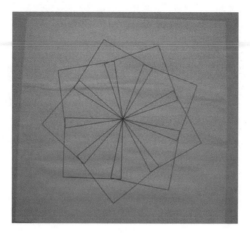

Figure 4.19   *LOGO design*

A motion sensor such as Ranger can be used to extend the interpretation of distance–time graphs to speed/velocity–time graphs. It can also be used for mathematical modelling. For example, if a large ball is dropped under a motion sensor and the bounces are picked up by the sensor, a series of parabolas are shown on the resulting graph. Additionally, more than one Ranger could be set up to pick up motion from different positions, and the separate graphs overlaid on a screen.

When PIP is used in conjunction with Ranger, only straight line graphs are produced. Children could be asked to use the Repeat key to write a program that will produce, for example, a symmetrical graph.

Also, children can translate a sequence of commands into a numerical statement that corresponds to the distances travelled by PIP, measured from the starting point. For example, the following PIP instructions produce a spiky graph:

CM Repeat 5 Forward 50 Back 30 End Go

If PIP starts 20cm from the Ranger then, as a numerical statement, this could be written as $20 + 5(50 - 30) = 120$. This shows that after the sequence of moves, PIP is 120cm from the starting point. Children can make connections between the different representations: sequence of commands, graph and numerical statement.

Summary of Key Ideas

- Programmable floor devices such as PIP are more than just toys; they provide opportunities for play that lead to genuine problem solving and mathematical learning.
- Children can lead their own learning through the exploration of PIP and Ranger by asking and trying out their own 'What if...?' questions.
- Children test their ideas, receive immediate feedback and refine their 'solutions' as they watch PIP move or analyse a distance–time graph of motion in front of the Ranger.
- Collaboration and discussion are fostered as children plan and revise their ideas together.
- The role of the teacher changes from information provider to guide, since the children can pursue their own questions and suggestions.
- Children's exploration with floor robots and data loggers can motivate those who are less keen on 'maths' but more technically minded.

Pause for Reflection

■ What cross-curricular topics would lend themselves to the use of PIP and/or Ranger?

■ How might you introduce the idea of angle as a measure of turn using children themselves and a programmable floor device?

■ When you introduce PIP (or other floor devices) how much direction would you give and how much would you allow the children to explore?

■ How will you support children in keeping track of instructions since there is no screen display on PIP?

■ How would you organise your classroom when using PIP and/or Ranger? Would you prefer group work, whole class work or a mix of both?

Further Reading

Siraj-Blatchford, J. and Whitebread, D. (2003) *Supporting Information and Communications Technology in the Early Years*. Maidenhead: Open University Press.
  Chapter 4 (pp. 42–59) 'Programmable Toys and Control Technology' gives a detailed overview of the benefits of using control technology and describes some examples for use in the classroom.

Way, J. and Beardon, T. (eds) (2003) *ICT and Primary Mathematics*. Maidenhead: Open University Press.
  This is a very readable book. The authors enthusiastically describe how ICT can offer environments for learning mathematics in qualitatively different ways from traditional methods.

References

Hunscheidt, D. and Peter-Koop, A. (2006) *Tools rather than toys: fostering mathematical understanding through ICT in primary mathematics classrooms*. Paper presented at ICMI Study 17, Technology Revisited, Vietnam, Dec. 2006.

Papert, S. (1980) *Mindstorms: Children, Computers and Powerful Ideas*. New York: Basic Books.

Siraj-Blatchford, J. and Whitebread, D. (2003) *Supporting Information and Communications Technology in the Early Years*. Maidenhead: Open University Press.

Vincent. J. (2003) 'Learning Technologies'. In J. Way and T. Beardon (eds) *ICT and Primary Mathematics*. Maidenhead: Open University Press.

CHAPTER 5

Investigating Mathematical Reasoning and Decision Making

Milan Hejný and Jana Slezáková

Communicating the Theme

> Five-year-old twins – Andrew and Bethany – have been told to tidy up. Andrew bundles his toys into a green bag and Bethany puts hers into a yellow one. When their mother comes in to check how they are getting on there are still various items on the carpet – a ball, a skipping rope and a hoop – all of which their aunty gave them. The children are arguing about whose bag these toys belong in. Andrew suggests putting the ball into his bag since Bethany's bag is fuller. Bethany says that she plays with the ball more than Andrew hence it should be in her bag. Finally Bethany turns to their mother and announces, 'Mum, have a look, we need one more bag to put these toys in'.

In the illustration above, we can see some of the reasoning and decision making children might encounter in their everyday lives. Both children were discussing the matter intelligently and endeavouring to find practical solutions to their predicament. Bethany's solution is a wonderful compromise decision.

The illustration indicates the focus of this chapter. The starting point is an analysis of some of the situations frequently experienced by primary children in their everyday lives. In doing so we will show how a need to organise a set of objects or phenomena can lead to motivationally attractive and cognitively stimulating situations suitable for both the development of reasoning and decision making.

We begin by introducing our ideas with a classroom scene. Over the course of three days the following conversations took place between Cindy, Dan and their teacher.

Day 1

Teacher: Imagine we have two bags A and B. The numbers 2 and 8 are in bag A and the numbers 11 and 13 are in bag B. Put the number 12 into one of the bags and justify your decision.

(As the teacher says this, she writes 'A = {2, 8} B = {13, 11}' on the board.)

Cindy: 12 should go into bag A as it is an even number.
Dan: No, 12 belongs to bag B as it is a two-digit number.
Teacher: 12 belongs to bag B. Where do you think 26 might go?
Dan: Bag B.
Teacher: No, it belongs to the bag A.

At this point both children looked puzzled.

Teacher: 62 and 44 belong to bag A and the numbers 31 and 81 belong to bag B.

(As she says this she writes 'A = {2, 8, 26, 62, 44}, B = {13, 11, 12, 31, 81}' on the board.)

Cindy: Does that mean if the digit 1 is in the number, it is in the bag B, otherwise it is in the bag A?
Teacher: Exactly! Well done. That was my secret criterion for deciding which numbers should go into which bag.

Day 2

Teacher: Today we shall be working with three bags and, at the moment they each have three numbers in them. Your tasks are to decide where to put the numbers 4, 65 and 300 and explain your reasoning.

(She writes 'B1 = {13, 22, 31}, B2 = {101, 353, 671}, B3 = {3, 6, 9} on the board.)

Cindy and Dan set to work and rapidly found a solution, which Dan explained.

Dan: 4 belongs to B3 since it is a one-digit number, 65 belongs to B1 as it is a two-digit number and 300 belongs to B2 as it's a three-digit number.
Teacher: Great! You have found one solution very quickly. Would you be able to find another solution?

This proved more difficult but, after several attempts:

Cindy: 300 should be in B3 since it is divisible by 3 as are 3, 6 and 9.
Teacher: Excellent! Let me give you a hint: What is the remainder when you divide 13 by 3?
Dan: Ah! 4 belongs to B1 because if you divide any of the numbers by 3 the remainder is always 1 and 65 should go into B2 since the remainder of all the numbers is 2 when they are divided by 3.

Day 3

Teacher: Today I want you to put the following six words – rabbit, sheep elephant, robin, swallow, eagle – into a 3 x 2 grid in a 'nice' way.

After some discussion the pupils create the following grid:

rabbit	sheep	elephant
robin	swallow	eagle

Table 5.1   Cindy and Dan's grid

Cindy: In the top row there are animals and in the bottom row there are birds. In the first column words start with 'r', in the second column words start with 's' and in the last column words start with 'e'.

Dan: We thought of other solutions. For example we can exchange the first and the second row or the first and the third column.

In this chapter we will provide a range of class, group and paired activities which can help individuals improve their ability to classify and, in doing so, provide entertaining and effective ways to exercise and enhance different mental abilities. The central idea involves the game 'Guess and Pay'. All these activities have been used successfully with children and adults both in the Czech Republic and the other COSIMA countries.

Communicating the Concepts

'Guess and Pay' may be unfamiliar to readers and therefore we will introduce it through various examples. Eddie and Frank were asked to display the following six cards on a 3 x 2 grid in any logical way they wished: ◎,△,▣,◎,△,▢. The result of their work is given in Table 5.2.

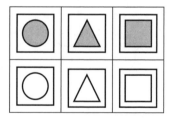

Table 5.2   Eddie and Frank's first grid

When asked, Eddie explained that the top row included all the blue shapes (shown as shaded in Table 5.2) and that the bottom row was all white. The following conversation then took place.

Teacher: Is it possible to remove ◎ from the grid?
Frank: Then there would be an extra card in the shaded row.
Teacher: Okay! but what if I didn't insist on there being the same number of cards in each row, would it be possible then?

Both children agreed that it would then be possible.

Teacher:	Would it be okay to add at least one of the following objects to the grid: Shaded star, white scooter and green triangle?
Frank:	No.
Eddie:	No.
Teacher:	Just remind me about the top row of cards again please.
Eddie:	It is the one for a shaded circle, a shaded triangle and shaded square.
Frank:	In other words it is the row for shaded ones.
Eddie:	Okay. So, yes, the shaded star can be added to the row.
Teacher:	Do you agree Frank?
Frank:	If the shaded star had been among the cards at the beginning, then okay…We could classify the first row as 'all shaded' and the second one 'all white'.

The children then decided to add a third row and classify it as 'all green' so that it could accommodate the green triangle the teacher had suggested previously. Frank added that you could also add 'grass' to such a row.

This example illustrates the importance of mathematical classifications and how one can sometimes add new – and often completely unexpected – objects. Thus, for example, you might be astonished to find a year 1 child who struggled with counting up to 20 adding '100', or even, '$\frac{1}{2}$' to a row of numbers. Similarly we might be surprised if a primary student-teacher included a non-convex quadrilateral with diagonals that do not cross alongside a square and a rectangle in their row of quadrilateral shapes. From a teacher's perspective, this extension process is very important as this is one way the pupils acquire, and demonstrate, new knowledge. For this reason, it is unwise to limit the classification process to grids of a specified size. Rather it is beneficial to encourage children to extend their grids to include additional objects which meet their chosen criteria. We call this extension process the extension of the universal set. This is a set of all objects (not only those supplied by the teacher) meeting the condition of the given criterion. For example in Figure 5.1, the universal sets were all shaded and all white objects. This idea will be discussed more fully later in the chapter.

Picture George (aged eight years, one month) and Henry (aged seven years and 6 months) in a year 3 classroom. They have already had experience of solving classification problems with one criterion. They were given a blank grid with 3 x 2 boxes and the following six cards:

Figure 5.1   *Hens, cats and dogs*

Initially George distributed the cards as shown in Table 5.3 saying, 'This is the shaded row and this is the white one.' Without a word, Henry switched the white cat and the white hen. On seeing this George exclaimed, 'Yes!'.

Shaded hen	Shaded cat	Shaded dog
White cat	White hen	White dog

Table 5.3   *George and Henry's first task*

Teacher: Why did you exchange them Henry?

Henry (pointing to the first and the second columns of the grid): So that we can have hens here and cats there!

Teacher: Okay, are you up for an even trickier task?
Boys: Yes!

The teacher gave them a grid 4 x 3 and asked them how many cards would they need to fill it. They both answered 12 correctly. The teacher then gave them the following set of 12 cards (which we will call the gallery of the game from now on):

G(1) ={ ⊡ ⊞ ⊙ ⊕ ◾ ⊞ ⬤ ⊕ ▪ ⊞ ⊙ ⊕ }

She placed two cards into two empty boxes of the grid.

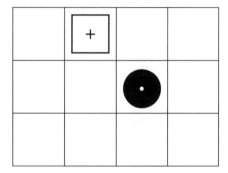

Table 5.4   George and Henry's second task

The teacher then challenged the boys to put the remaining ten cards into the grid, 'in a nice way.' George opted for the colour criterion initially, but agreed with certain suggestions made by Henry concerning the shapes. After that he also attended to the shape of the cards as he put them into the grid. The work was quick and in 29 seconds the boys came to the following conclusion:

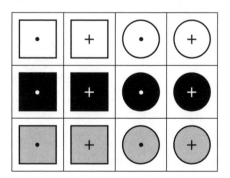

Table 5.5   George and Henry's response to their second challenge

In other words, building on the teacher's positioning of only two cards, the boys were able to place the remaining cards into the grid so that those in every row met one criterion (i.e. colour) while those in every column met another (i.e. shape).

Now we are ready to introduce Guess and Pay. The game is designed for at least two players – a Guesser and a Payee. The Payee begins by constructing a grid of m x n boxes (e.g. in Table 5.5 m = 4 and n = 3) and places a card in each box in such a way that the cards in each row meet one criterion while those in the columns meet another. (You can use objects instead of cards if you wish.)

Having done this, the Payee gives the Guesser an empty m x n grid and a duplicate set of cards. The Guesser's task is to place the cards in the empty grid in the same way as the Payee. The Guesser can ask three types of questions:

1. In which box will I find this card (pointing to a certain card from his/her collection)?
2. Which card is in this box (pointing to a specific box on the grid)?
3. Is this card in this box (pointing to a specific card and box)?

The Payee will answer any of the above questions but the Guesser has to pay for each answer. The price for answers to questions of types 1 and 2 is five points but only one point for type 3 questions. The Guesser's task is to find the solution and pay as little as possible.

Let's illustrate the game with an example: Irene (the Payee) has prepared the same grid as the one in Table 5.6. Jane (the Guesser) has an empty 4 x 3 grid in front of her and a duplicate copy of the cards Irene used, randomly arranged on the desk. The following discussion takes place:

Jane: What is in this box? (pointing to the box in the upper left hand corner)
Irene (pointing to ⊡): I need to put down five points for that.
Jane placed ⊡ in the upper left hand box of her grid.
Irene: What is in this box? (pointing to the bottom right hand box.)
Irene pointed to ⊕ and wrote down another five points.

Jane put the second card into her grid and after a pause she placed more cards into the grid as shown in Table 5.6.

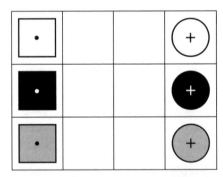

Table 5.6   *Jane's partial solution*

Jane: Are squares with pluses in this column (pointing to the second column)?
Irene: You can't ask that sort of question. It's not allowed.
Jane: Does this card ⊙ go into the box next to this one ⊡ ?
Irene: No. (writing down '1' point):
Jane: Then, this one must (pointing to ⊞).

She then quickly – and successfully – completed the whole grid and the game was over. Jane finished with the same grid as Irene and it cost her 11 points in total.

When the game was over the girls tried to find another way to sort the same collection of cards. This time Jane was the Payee and Irene was the Guesser. They discovered that, with a bit of good luck, it was possible for Irene to solve the task paying only ten points.

In years 4 and 5, when pupils have had experience with two-criteria classification and with Guess and Pay, the teacher can set up two types of competitions. Either the teacher is the Payee and the pupils are divided into groups to guess the teacher's solution, or groups of pupils participate in a tournament in which every group plays another group, first as the Payees and then as Guessers. To organise the tournament and to prevent any misunderstandings, it is necessary to prepare clear instructions beforehand. A set of such instructions made by some of the project teachers can be found on the accompanying DVD (Item 5.1: Guess and Pay Rules).

Communicating Experiences with Pre-service Teachers

In this section, we will describe the ways in which our pre-service teachers were introduced to the game Guess and Pay. In essence, they obtained their experience through four different activities.

1. They played Guess and Pay between themselves or with us, teachers.
2. They analysed several games together and tried to find the optimal solution for the Guesser.
3. They made scenarios for playing the game in mathematics classes.
4. They implemented the scenarios in classes.

The following illustrations will explain the process. One game played by pre-service teachers – Irene and Jane – was described above. We will now describe how another pair – Kate and Lucy – tried to find the optimal solution for a grid 3 x 2 and gallery G(2) = {◻▲◻●▲■}. The students gradually analysed two strategies and then compared their suitability. To be able to describe the students' thinking meaningfully, we will denote the six boxes of the grid with the letters A to F as follows:

A	B	C
D	E	F

Table 5.7   *Letters*

This is the discussion which took place:

Kate: I would start with the question – What is in box A?
Lucy: Okay. Let us assume that there is a white circle.

(Lucy places the object ◻ into box A.)

Lucy: Well, and what if there is something else? … Oh yes, it would continue in the same way.
Kate: 'Cause, it doesn't matter if there is something else.
Lucy: So, if the white circle is here…
Kate: White must be here and here (points to boxes B and C).
Lucy: And all three black objects are on the second row.

Kate: It means we have to ask just one question more. What about 'Is the white triangle here in B?'.

Lucy: If 'yes', triangles are in the second column and squares are the third column. If 'no', triangles are in the third column and squares in the second column.

Kate: Therefore this problem can be solved in six points.

The teacher asked whether the first question was necessary. This made Lucy and Kate think about another strategy. Their second strategy assumes that they will ask only one point questions.

Kate: I would try to put all of the objects into box A, one by one. So, the first question would be 'Is the white circle in box A?'

Lucy: If 'yes', we'd be lucky and only have to pay two points for the solution.

Kate: If 'no', we would ask 'Is the white triangle in box A'?'

Lucy: If 'yes', we would have to pay three points for the solution.

Kate: Correct. If 'no', we would ask 'Is the white square in box A?'

Lucy: It's pretty clear. Finally we would find which object goes into box A and, at most, we would have to pay six points for it. This would be only in the case if this object is the black square.

Kate: No, no. We do not need to ask the last question. If the answer is 'no' five times then it is pretty clear that in box A must be the last object – the black square.

Lucy: Excellent. So, this way of asking is better than the previous one. Using this solving strategy we will not have to pay more than 6 points, but in many cases it will be less.

The teacher was satisfied with the students' solution and gave them another gallery:

$$G(3) = \{ \odot\ \boxed{\star}\ \triangle\ \boxed{+}\ \triangle\ \circledcirc \}.$$

Lucy immediately said that it does not matter if the gallery is this one or the previous one. The solving strategy must be same. The teacher did not comment this idea. She just repeated that tomorrow they would play the game with this gallery. The student teachers decided to look closer at the new gallery.

Kate: Well, we can create a grid. Let me see.

She then created Table 5.8a.

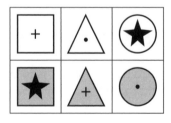

Table 5.8a   *Kate's solution 1*

Lucy: No, these two stars should be in one column and these two pluses in another column and...

Kate: Oh yes, you are right. It is a tricky gallery. You can do it in completely different ways. Let me draw it.

She then created Table 5.8b.

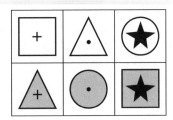

Table 5.8b   *Lucy's solution 2*

Lucy:	So, this gallery is an exceptional one. To solve this you have to ask about each object.
Kate:	I wouldn't say that. If we know that the white square is in box A – as we have it in both grids – we know in the first row there are white surrounds and in the second row shaded surrounds objects. Do you agree?
Lucy:	Possibly. I am a bit confused. I don't like galleries like this much.
Kate:	Okay, we are tired. Let's go for cup of coffee.

This was the end of the solving process for the two student teachers at this stage. Later on Kate found that in fact the problem was not so difficult. She solved it and explained her solution to Lucy thus:

Kate:	Suppose there is a white square in the box A with the inner sign '+'. We know that this would cost us less than six points. Now there are just two possibilities for the object in D: either shaded square with the inner sign '★' or shaded triangle with the inner sign '+'. To find it, it will cost one point. And now we are in fact finished. In the first case the solution is here [she points to Table 5.8a.] and in the second case the solution is here [she points to Table 5.8b].
Lucy:	Wait, wait. How do you know that in this box [She points to box B] there is a white triangle? Couldn't a white circle go there?
Kate:	Oh, yes. These two columns are not clear yet. We need one more question to fix them.
Lucy:	So, am I correct saying that for this gallery, in the worse case scenario, we would need seven points?
Kate:	I think so.

Lucy drew Tables 5.9c and 5.9d.

Kate:	Yes, so if we suppose that the white square is in box A we know that there are four possibilities – these two she points to Tables 5.8a and 5.8b. and these two She points to Tables 5.8c and 5.8d.

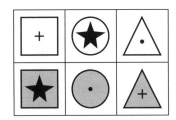

Table 5.8c   *Lucy's solution 3*

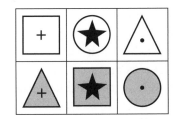

Table 5.8d   *Lucy's solution 4*

Lucy:	I am curious to know if the teacher has even more difficult galleries than this one.

When Lucy asked the teacher for a more demanding gallery for a 3 x 2 grid, the teacher answered: 'Mmm, that's an interesting question. I'm afraid I don't know the answer. See if you can find out'. (See DVD Item 5.5: Galleries.)

The process of finding strategies for larger grids is more demanding and appealed to only a few of the more mathematically oriented student teachers. Most of the other student teachers focused on the creation of scenarios and galleries which could be used in primary mathematics classes. They experimented with many of the galleries they created themselves. Many of them can be found on the accompanying DVD (see Item 5.2: Other galleries).

Here are two examples of galleries, created by student teachers, which can be organised according to more than two criteria:

$$G(4) = \{ \ \boxdot \ \blacksquare \ \boxtimes \ \blacksquare \ \odot \ \oplus \ \circledast \ \odot \ \triangle \ \triangle \ \blacktriangle \ \triangle \ \}$$

$$G(5) = \{776, 865, 954, 2277, 2593, 4448\}$$

The last gallery was created by a very clever student teacher – Martin – and was presented in the following way: Find as many grids as possible using the gallery ensuring that the number 776 is in the box A. After two weeks his classmates found the following two solutions:

776	865	954
4448	2593	2277

Table 5.9a *Solution 1*

776	954	4448
2277	2593	865

Table 5.9b *Solution 2*

The solver who created Table 5.9a explained: In the first row there are three-digit numbers, in the second row four-digit numbers. The sum of digits of numbers in the first column is 20, in the second column it is 19 and in the third column it is 18.

The solver who created Table 5.9b explained: In the first row there are even numbers, in the second row odd numbers. If the digit 7 is in the number it belongs to the first column, if the digit 9 is in the number it belongs to the second column and if the digit 8 is in the number it belongs to the third column.

Martin announced that there is one more solution which was yet to be found (see DVD Item 5.8: Analysis of more demanding problems).

Communicating Activities for the Classroom

A simplified version of the Guess and Pay game can be played in year 1. The higher the year, the more challenging the game can become. However, it is not possible to introduce the game without pupils first learning about the classification process. Generally speaking, Guess and Pay can be implemented following two preparatory stages. In the first stage, the children are introduced with one criterion classification. The second stage involves two-criterion classification. Each stage is presented as a game.

The first game is called 'Place into the Right Bag' and it was illustrated earlier in the chapter with Table 5.1. The following three games took place in a year 2 class in the czech Republic. The pupils were between seven- and eight-years-old.

Illustration 1

The teacher drew the outline of a table on the board and marked two columns: the left one was headed 'blue bag' and the right one 'yellow bag'. Under both bags, he added three names. Under that he wrote the name Peggy and asked the children where he should place Peggy (see Table 5.10a). They answered that it should go into the blue bag because 'There are girls in the blue bag and boys in the yellow bag.'

Blue bag	Yellow bag
Ella Nicola Fay	Edgar George Eric
Peggy	

Table 5.10a *Bags*

Comment: All children understood this classification without any problems. It allowed the teacher to start on a more demanding problem.

Illustration 2

The teacher erased the names from Table 5.10a and put Edgar, George, and Nicola in the blue bag and Ella, Jill, and Ann in the yellow bag (Table 5.10b).

Blue bag	Yellow bag
Edgar George Nicola	Ella Jill Ann
Peggy	

Table 5.10b *Bags*

He asked the pupils the same question as before, 'In which bag should we put Peggy?' This task was more complicated. However Nina found a solution.

Nina: Peggy is yellow, since you have 'gg' there. In Ella you have 'll', so you have in Jill and 'nn' in Ann.

Teacher: Very good! It is one possibility. But in fact Peggy is in the blue bag, not in the yellow one.

The teacher put Peggy's name into the left column and wrote the name Joe as a new question. The pupils were surprised. And for a long time no suggestions were put forward. So, the teacher put 'Joe' into the right column and asked the children to offer other names for him to classify. In this way, he put the names Helen, Samuel, and Frank in the blue bag. On the other hand, he put the names Noel and Mary in the yellow bag (see Table 5.10c).

Blue bag	Yellow bag
Edgar	Ella
George	Jill
Nicola	Ann
Peggy	Joe
Helen	Noel
Samuel	Mary
Frank	

Table 5.10c   Bags

Oliver (shouting): In the yellow bag, there are short names, and in the blue one, there are long ones!

Patrick: Yes, you are right. But would you be able to say more precisely which names are long and which are short?

Nina: Four letters is short, and five is long.

Oliver: Three letters is also short. Six letters is long.

Patrick: And what about me? I have seven letters.

Nina (counted the letters of Patrick's name on her fingers): You will be in another bag.

This was followed by a long and rich discussion facilitated by the teacher although he found no need to contribute in terms of content. Some of the pupils reacted aggressively while the others tried to find a compromise. It ended with Oliver's and Nina's suggestions.

Oliver: In the blue bag there are names with two, three, and four letters. And all other names are in the yellow bag.

Nina: I would put very long names to a green bag.

The teacher observed that majority of the pupils agreed either with Oliver's or with Nina's solution.

Comment. The above illustration demonstrates how classification tasks can stimulate lively discussion between children leaving the teacher to observe and manage the conversation without significant intervention. In the discussion which took place in the class, the process of finding the solution to the classification problem was not the only objective. The social phenomena of the assertion of the more aggressive pupils' opinions are also very important. The teacher's encouragement of the less assertive pupils contributed to the development of their communication skills and the fostering of their social behaviour. It needs to be stated that the teacher had been teaching this particular class for more than 18 months and the pupils knew that he valued their ideas and discussions.

Illustration 3

One week later. The teacher wrote Table 5.11 on the board.

Blue bag	Yellow bag
31, 17, 19 10	68, 38, 89, 78
18	

Table 5.11   Bags

He asked the children whether number 18 should go into the blue or the yellow bag. Nina said that 18 should go into the yellow bag, as there were all numbers with digit 8. The teacher asked the rest of the class if she was right. They agreed. Only Patrick said that number 18 could go into the blue bag also, as all the numbers in it included the digit 1. Once again discussion followed, which lasted for 20 minutes. There were many suggestions and finally the pupils came up with the following conclusion: there should be two more bags, a green one for numbers with both the digits 1 and 8, and a red one for numbers containing neither of them.

All three illustrations are closely connected with two class (bag) classification. We saw that the pupils wanted to extend the number of bags. In classes where this idea is not raised it is recommended the teacher present three or more class classification problems. For example, ask children to divide animals into birds, fish, insects and mammals; to classify means of transport according to the number of wheels (for example, ship and elevator with zero wheels, bicycles with two wheels, cars with four wheels); words according to the number of letters, and so on. Such cross-curricular activities are ideal catalysts for stimulating discussions: we observed a lively debate on whether a penguin is a bird or not. A further type of task which can promote class discussion is illustrated below.

Illustration 4

In a year 5 class – where all the pupils had considerable experience with the game Guess and Pay and created various galleries for themselves – Robert came up with the gallery: G(6) = {8, 9, 54, 81, 323, 512}. He placed number 9 in the top right box, number 512 into the bottom left box. His classmates quite quickly found the solution in Table 5.12a. Sally, who enjoys solving combinatorial problems with the sum of digits, came up with a different solution (see Table 5.12b).

	Number is even	Number is odd	Sum of digits is 8	Sum of digits is 9
1-digit	8	9	8	9
2-digit	54	81		54, 81
3-digit	512	323	323, 512	

Table 5.12a   *Classmates' solution 1*   *Table 5.12b*   *Sally's solution*

Robert (objecting): It is not the right solution, as some boxes are crowded and some of them are empty.

Sally (defending herself): My solution is also right because it divides the gallery into two halves.

	Number is even	Number is odd	Sum of ciphers is 8	Sum of ciphers is 9
1-digit	8	9	8	9
2-digit	54	71	71	54
3-digit	512	333	512	333

Table 5.12c   *Sally's solution 1* *Table 5.12d*   *Sally's solution 2*

After a short discussion, the teacher let the children vote. The winning opinion was that the table is filled in correctly only if there is only one number in each box. In spite of this, the teacher praised Sally and said that any table with one number in each box is called regular. He added that it would be possible to play such a game with cards distributed irregularly as had been suggested by Sally. The next day Sally came in with an adjusted version of Robert's gallery $G(7) = \{8, 9, 54, 71, 333, 512\}$. She replaced 81 with 71 and 323 with 333. Sally then explained that if she put 9 and 512 in the same boxes as Robert it will not be possible to solve her gallery immediately. She proved her assertion using Tables 5.12c and 5.12d.

We have described how to introduce the classification process to pupils using two classification criteria and prepare them for playing the game Guess and Pay. For year 1 and year 2 pupils, it is sensible to use semantic galleries only. Later these can be followed by galleries with geometrical shapes and then, finally, arithmetic galleries. The children who understand the concept of classification and know how to distribute regular galleries using two criteria are ready to solve problems with a specific gallery, some of the objects from the gallery being placed into the table initially. See the task presented in Table 5.4 above.

Experience in both Czech Republic and the UK suggests that children who start to create their own galleries are sufficiently prepared to play Guess and Pay with their peers. The following presents some interesting phenomena.

Illustration 5

A year 5 pupil, Tom, played Guess and Pay with Tony using the following gallery $G(8) = \{P, B, G, PINK, BLUE, GREEN\}$ and a 3 x 2 grid. Tom solved Tony's grid and paid seven points to produce Figure 5.2a. (When the pupils created their tasks they knew that they would probably play Guess and Pay via email with pupils in England or Germany. Therefore they tried to choose English words or internationally understandable signs or symbols.)

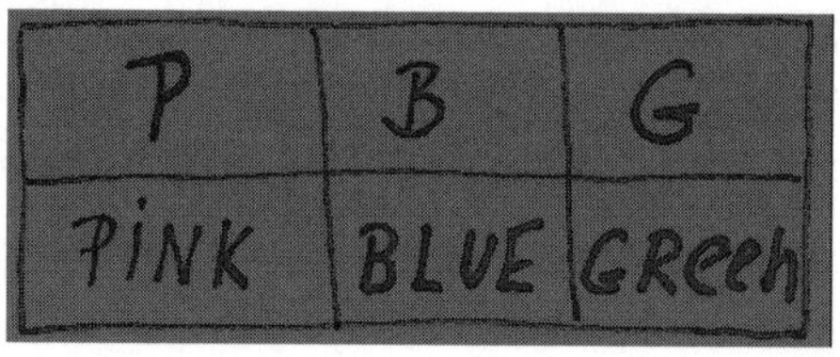

Figure 5.2a   *Tom's gallery*

The task had been solved but the children were not aware that the solution was problematic. The teacher therefore encouraged them to reflect on the matter by asking them for the name of the first bag/column. Tom said there was only letter P. The teacher asked him why 'pink' was in the bag. They answered that the first letter of the word is P. The teacher wondered whether the boys regarded the first column as a class of objects or just as a pair of two associated objects. So he decided to conduct a little experiment. He asked , 'Could the words for example 'purple' and 'Prague' go into the first bag or not?' Initially the children rejected this idea but later they discussed the question and finally they agreed: 'Yes, they could. This bag is for all English words starting with P.'

The teacher was glad that the boys were able to correct their apparently unclear understanding of the concept of classification. In the quest to support the boys' new understanding the teacher added two more rows to the grid and wrote 'Prague' with 'pig' beneath it (Figure. 5.2b). He asked the pupils to complete the remaining four boxes. This task was solved without any problems with words 'Berlin', 'Glasgow', 'bull' and 'goat'.

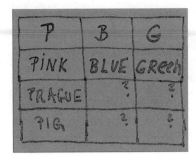

Figure 5.2b   New rows

Comment. Initially neither boy appreciated the *classes* of objects in the columns but only pairs of associated objects: P – PINK, B – BLUE, G – GREEN. The teacher found an effective way to lead the boys to a deeper understanding using only suitable questions so that they could recognise that in each column there is a class of objects and not only a pair. Similar situations can be seen below in Figures 5.3, 5.4, 5.5.

The confusion between classifications and associations was a quite frequent error particularly when playing with 2 x 3 or 2 x 4 grids. This was one of the most frequent errors made by the student teachers. The re-educational strategy described above and illustrated in Figure 5.2b is called 'the extension of the table'.

Every teacher knows that if something is discovered by a class, it does not mean every pupil understands it. Association errors will occur all the time and it is a question of time and a teachers' patience to eliminate their occurrence. Some of the pupils' galleries can be seen in Figures 5.3 to 5.11. All the children – the authors of the galleries – are year 5 pupils, except the creator of Figure 5.3 who was in year 3. As you will note some of the grids are fine, others are more problematic and some are totally wrong. The following figures represent the most frequent results we observed.

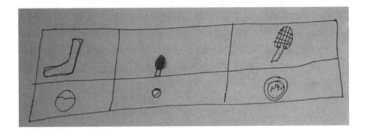

Figure 5.3   *Ball games*

This gallery is connected with ball games. In the bottom row there are pictures of balls (football, table tennis, tennis), and in the top row there are objects to get the balls rolling (foot, bat, racquet). Again, it is probable that the author (a year 3 pupil) does not think of the columns as classes but only as associated pairs. A teacher can determine whether this is the case by asking the author to extend the grid. Most common in such situations is that the children extend the grid by adding another column and not another row. In such case the teacher might use 'the extension of the table' strategy: ask the solver to add the third row to the table (it might be a row of three words: football, table tennis, tennis).

Figure 5.4   *Arithmetic association*

This picture is another example of the association, this time arithmetic. Here, as in the previous example, the teacher might deepen the author's understanding by asking them to extend the grid by one or more rows. Also in this case a teacher might use 'the extension of the table' strategy: ask the solver to add a third row to the table (for example, a row of three expressions: 20 + 20, 10 + 20, 10 + 10).

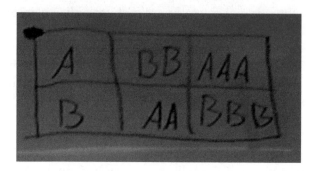

Figure 5.5   *Letters 1*

The gallery in Figure 5.5 has been placed in the grid to meet the column criterion (in the first column there is one letter, in the second two letters, etc.) but the row criterion has not been met. In each row, there are both the letters A and B. Thus the grid has been completed incorrectly. If we swapped the cards in the top and the bottom boxes in the middle column, the grid would be correct. The same error was made by other authors (see below). Often this error occurs when the authors are distracted by an aesthetic criterion. In the above case, the aesthetic criterion was a chess pattern of the cards type A and B. The advantage of this kind of grid is the fact that it can be extended in both directions.

Figure 5.6   *Letters 2*

Essentially Figure 5.6 illustrates the same phenomenon: only instead of letter B there is letter C. In this case, the grid is completed incorrectly, as neither the column nor the row criterion is respected. The author explained his aesthetic principle saying, 'The Cs go into the left top part and the As to the right bottom part.'

Figure 5.7   Numbers

The author of this grid did not understand the essence of classification. Similar grids frequently occur when working with year 1 pupils. Here each row comprises a sequence of even numbers. The numbers in the top row are two bigger than the numbers in the bottom row. While there is a certain organisation of the cards, it is by no means a classification. With the given objects {2, 4, 4, 6, 6, 8} it is impossible to make a regular grid. The same objects (two 2s and two 6s) must be in the same box regarding any criterion.

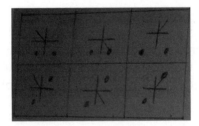

Figure 5.8   Line segments and dots

This is a very nice task in which every object is made of three elements. The first element is the cross, which is common to all the objects. The second element is the line segment starting in the centre of the cross and heading up to the left, down to the right or up to the right. The third object is a pair of dots placed horizontally or diagonally. The line segment is the criterion dividing objects into three classes and the two dots is the criterion dividing the objects into two classes. The cross is not a criterion as it is common to all the objects.

Figure 5.9   Shape and filling

Again, a nice and correct task. The row criterion is the shape (i.e. triangular and square). The column criterion is the filling (i.e. dots, horizontal and vertical hatching).

Figure 5.10   Numbers and filling

The author of this grid also did Figure 5.9. His intention was to modify the idea of the previous task and instead of geometry (i.e. triangle and square) to use arithmetic (i.e. the numbers 10 and 20). Due to an absent minded moment, he put 10 instead of 20 into the second row and therefore the grid is incorrect.

Figure 5.11   *Traffic signs*

This is one of the most original semantic tasks we observed. The basic idea lies in the polarity of some of the traffic signs when one traffic sign prohibits, directs or limits something, while the other lifts the restrictions. It is clear that the grid 3 x 2 could be extended to 4 x 2 or 5 x 2 using the above criterion. The question of whether it is possible to extend the grid to 3 x 3 is left up to you, the readers!

Communicating Ideas for In-service Courses

The authors of the book organised several workshops focusing on reasoning and decision making for teachers in the Czech Republic (from 2004 to 2006), Slovakia (2004), Germany (2005 and 2006) and Hungary (2005). In Slovakia, two 2-day courses for teachers took place. The courses were given as workshops. The teachers, in pairs, began by solving the given problems and then they devised their own tasks. Following this, they analysed pupils' solutions previously collected by colleagues. We will briefly describe the lessons learnt from the courses. At the end of this section we will present a very nice and original task created by German teachers.

From the outset, it was apparent that the teachers did not have a clear idea about the formal mathematical concepts of classification, classification criterion and class. To help them understand these ideas, we found that metaphoric language seemed to be effective. Instead of the word 'class' we used the word 'bag' and instead of 'classification criterion' we used 'name of bag'. Using the metaphorical language, the formal mathematical statement '48 goes to the classes determined by the criterion of even numbers' was modified to '48 goes to the bag labelled even numbers'.

In the first stage of our workshop – when the participants were solving given problems – they tended to make two types of error. Take Groups A and B who were asked to classify children's names. They both produced the same solution:

Alice	Anthony	Audrey
Bernard	Boris	Brenda
Cedric	Cindy	Clement
Daniel	Deborah	Dolly

Table 5.13   *Names*

A representative of group A explained how they had reached their solution.

Ursula: In the rows, there are names starting with letters A, B, C, and D. In the columns, there is always one name starting with the given letter.

A representative of group B was not fully satisfied with Ursula's explanation. She addressed Ursula with the following objection:

Victoria: You do not explain into which column Alice should go, for example. By swapping Anthony with Alice, your column criterion would still work. How do you know that Alice belongs to the first column? We have a clear column criterion: the first column is for names which are first in alphabetical order, the second column for those which are second and so on.

This explanation was accepted as correct by the majority of the participants but then Ursula objected:

Ursula: It is not possible to name the bag 'first letter of the given trio'. You know we have been told that the allocation of the names cannot be dependent on the given gallery. If we had, for example, Barbara instead of Brenda, Bernard would have had to go into the second and not the first column.

The following discussion showed that understanding the idea of criterion of classification is quite demanding. The above debate was interrupted by an interesting proposition from Wendy:

Wendy: I would put names with five letters into the first column, names with six letters into the second and names with seven letters to the third.

After further discussion Wendy's solution was accepted by all participants.

Comment. There are two errors in the discussion described above. The first can be called 'replacement of classification with distribution'. The essence of this error is that the allocation of particular items is not clear. We know only that each column/bag requires one name starting with A, but we do not know precisely where to place 'Alice'. The second error is the 'incorrect use of seriation'. The essence of this mistake lies in pre-distribution of the whole gallery before the classification. In the above case it was the distribution of all of the items in alphabetical order, followed by placing the whole distributed sequence into the given grid. It became clear, however, that if one item was replaced by another, the whole sequence changed and it became necessary to reallocate the item in the grid.

In the second part of the seminar, the participants created their own classification problems for their pupils. It was interesting that the spectrum of the tasks made by children and by teachers were similar including the association errors. The most illustrative task made by one of the groups was the following gallery: ant, butterfly, flower, grass, squirrel, tree. The classification into two classes 'plants versus animals' is correct. However, linkages 'squirrel – tree', 'ant – grass', 'butterfly – flower' are associative rather than classificatory. Some solvers could not detect their mistake. One of the solvers suggested putting a label 'nest' on the bag, as she understood it as a linkage between the animal and the plant on which it lives.

Comment. The given tasks were made for year 1 pupils. We agreed with the authors of the tasks that they would be interesting for the children, recognising that the distinction between association and classification is so fine that such confusion cannot be considered to be wrong in year 1 and at primary level generally.

Finally, we presented a problem created by the German teachers (Figure. 5.12). There are units in the first row of measurement, and real objects closely connected with the particular unit in the second row. The third row contains one-word descriptions indicating how the unit is connected with the particular object. (Türbreite = door width, Milchtüte = milk carton, Fingerbreite = finger width, Mehlpackung = flour bag). The teaching point of the grid is evident. It is interesting that as in Figure 5.12, each column is based on an association and not a classification. The measurement units in the first row give the names to the columns. For example, '1 cm' is the name for the the third column. Similarly in Figure 5.2a, letter P was the name for the first column.

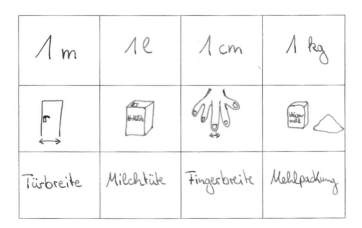

Figure 5.12   Physical units, real objects and description

Communicating Related Follow-up Activities

So far we have seen several galleries and their classifying criteria. More galleries and criteria can be found on the DVD. Below are some other suggestions for galleries and criteria. From many possibilities we have selected six areas: arithmetic, geometry, combinations and permutations, words, geography, and famous personalities. We believe that a reader can use our suggestions and adapt them according to his/her interest. We would like to add that creating galleries is an inspiring activity!

Arithmetic

We have already seen five types of criteria applied to natural numbers: number of digits, sum of digits, even/odd, remainder when divided by three, containing a given digit. Further criteria might be introduced by operations. This case is illustrated by galleries. See the list on the DVD Item 5.2, for example G(17) = {1 + 8, 3 + 5, 14 - 5, 11 - 3, 7 + 4, 13 - 2} and G(18) = {8 + 10, 3.7, 3.6, 12 + 9, 7 + 13, 4 . 5}.

2D Geometry

Besides the criterion of elementary shapes (square, triangle, circle, star, plus sign, dot) we can consider more demanding shapes (for example, right-angled triangle, isosceles trapezium, non-convex figure) and more demanding geometrical ideas such as area or perimeter. An illustration is the gallery:

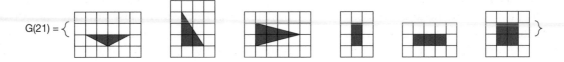

Shapes on square grid

(For criteria see DVD item 5.5.2)

3D Geometry

Here we can consider either the simplest solids like cube, prism, pyramid, sphere, cylinder, cone, or cube solids such as models for buildings. The illustration is given by gallery G(33) =

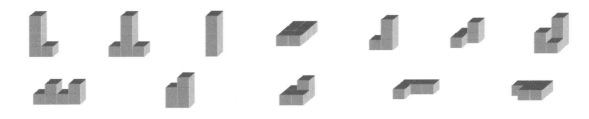

Cube solids

(For criteria see DVD Item 5.5.2.)

Combinations and permutations

The most demanding galleries can be found in this area. One such gallery is discussed here together with its criteria:

$$G(22) = \{ACgh, ACfj, ADei, BCeh, BDfi, BDgj\}$$

Here we have to consider two row criteria:

- the first capital A or B and the second capital C or D;
- two column criteria: the first small letter e, f, or g and the second small letter h, i, or j.

If we carefully look at the six objects of the gallery we can find that objects ACgh and BDfi cannot be in the same row since A ≠ B and C ≠ D. These objects cannot be in the same column either since g ≠ f and h ≠ i. Such pairs of objects will be called complementary. We can note that among the six given objects in this gallery there is just one complementary pair, namely ACgh and BDfi. Since these two objects must be in different rows and different columns we can restrict ourselves to solutions in which these two objects are firmly fixed (Figure 5.13a).

ACgh		
	BDfi	

Figure 5.13a *Letter clusters*

Combining row and column criteria we can theoretically obtain four different solutions (Figure 5.13b). It is not difficult to complete three of these tables. However the last one does not give a satisfactory solution (see Figure 5.13c).

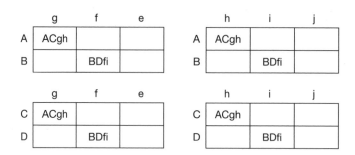

Figure 5.13b   *Solutions*

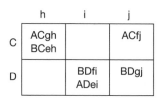

Figure 5.13c   *Solution 4*

It is surprising that this gallery (G(22)) from the point of its structure, is equal to the gallery G(5) = {776, 865, 954, 2277, 2593, 4448}. This is discussed more fully on the DVD (Item 5.5.8).

Words

We have already seen the criteria: the first letter of word and the number of letters in the word. However in these cases the second criteria was focused on the meaning of words. It is not too difficult to create galleries in which only the linguistic criteria are regarded. As an example we will take the gallery G(43) = {banana, bed, boat, crew, cutter, goose, screw, table, trainer}. (For criteria see DVD.)

Geography

A diversity of geographical terms (e.g. towns, states, rivers, lakes, mountains, regions) offers wide variety of interesting galleries. As an example we will take the gallery G(27) = {Berlin, London, Paris, Rhine, Seine, Thames}. (For criteria see DVD.)

Famous personalities

This area was the most attractive for some of our student teachers. They created a lot of galleries. Usually the first criterion concerned the personality's profession and the second criterion related to either their nationality or their period in history. One such gallery is G(36) = {Bach, Curie, Dürer, Goethe, Hugo, Mendelejev, Pushkin, Ravel, Renoir, Repin, Röntgen, Tchaikovsky}. (For criteria see DVD Item 5.5.2.)

Up until now we have discussed how to extend the game Guess and Pay into different areas. Now we turn our attention to an issue which arose from the game and involves probability theory.

When solving the task with G(2) Kate and Lucy considered two different strategies. In the first one – let us call it 'direct' – the first question cost 5 points. We saw that in this case the final solution cost 6 points. In the second strategy – let us call it 'one-by-one' – the total price of game was dependent on chance. In this case a lucky guesser might pay only 2 points and an unlucky guesser 6 points. If Kate and Lucy wanted to know what was the 'average' price of one game they could do an experiment. One of them could act as a payee and prepare ten different grids while the other took the part of guesser finding the solution using the one-by-one strategy. We did such experiment and found that ten games cost 5, 6, 2, 2, 6, 4, 3, 4, 5, 4 respectively. Thus the total price for ten games was 41 points making the average cost of a game 4.1 points.

The theoretical approach to finding the average price of one game using the one-by-one strategy is 13/3 points. A reader who is familiar with the elements of probability theory can find the result for him/herself. For your information we note that the lowest possible average price of the game with a grid 4 x 2 is 28/3 and the lowest possible average price of the game with grid 5 x 2 is 329/24.

Comment: Guess and Pay can be used as a highly motivating introduction to probability theory.

Summary of Key Ideas

- ◆ Decision making and mathematical reasoning are fundamental intellectual abilities.
- ◆ They can be developed in primary education in many different ways. The most efficient are those using the organisation of a set of objects with respect to different criteria.
- ◆ In traditional mathematics teaching the learning material is presented in an arranged and organised format. Situations when pupils are asked to organise a set of data are rather rare and exceptional.
- ◆ The game Guess and Pay and associated problems offer a rich spectrum of situations which help to develop classification skills.
- ◆ The diversity of the tasks offered by Guess and Pay allows teachers to set suitable problems for primary and secondary pupils and even future teachers.
- ◆ The best way to present Guess and Pay on in-service courses is to challenge teachers to be creative both in terms of the mathematics they use and the manner in which it is taught.
- ◆ The series of experiments discussed show that Guess and Pay situations foster children's communicative skills in both basic directions: articulation of their own ideas and interpretation of somebody else's ideas.

Pause for Reflection

- ■ Where can we meet classification in everyday life situations? (Shopping, household, means of transport, traffic signs, literature, music, sport, finance, scientific inventions and discoveries, geographical terminology …)
- ■ Where in everyday life can your pupils meet classification? (Toys, family, social games, food, school building, TV programmes, fairy tale creatures, calendar, professions …)
- ■ In which children's games do you find classification, distribution or association?
- ■ When have you used classification outside mathematics classes?
- ■ Take any mathematics textbook used by your pupils and find examples of classification there.
- ■ If we know the following five words of a gallery of nine – chirp, coat, cow, hiss, snakeskin – what might be the remaining words?
- ■ Do you like or dislike classification in mathematics and in everyday life? How would you characterise children with such preferences?
- ■ When have you used classification in teaching arithmetic and geometry?

From our experience, Guess and Pay brings children's thinking processes to the fore. It is interesting to observe that sometimes a first grader plays the game more effectively than a fifth grader and that the techniques discussed in this chapter allowed us to identify mathematically talented pupils.

Further Reading

Turner, S. and McCulloch, J. (2004) *Making Connections in Primary Mathematics*. London: David Fulton Publishers.

This is a very accessible book which discusses the value of understanding relationships in mathematics and hence why classification is such an important part of early learning. The authors explain their thinking using a range of mathematical and cross-curricular examples.

Haylock, D.H. and Cockburn, A.D. (2003) *Understanding Mathematics in the Lower Primary Years* (2nd edition). London: Sage Publications.

In Chapter 8 – 'Handling Data' – Derek Haylock and Anne Cockburn clearly explain the importance of teaching children classification in the early years of schooling. They provide a range of interesting examples ready for classroom use.

Brown, L., Reid, D.A. and Coles, A. (2003) Seeing patterns: somatic markers in teachers' decision-making and students' reasoning in mathematics classrooms. In S. Pope and O. McNamara (eds), *Research in Mathematics Education: Volume 5*. London: The British Society for Research into Learning Mathematics.

Using two transcripts of classroom conversations, Laurinda Brown and her colleagues demonstrate that decision making in classrooms often takes place without time for reflection. They argue that encouraging children to make their decisions more consciously will improve performance and guide their future actions.

Schwartz, S.L. (2005) *Teaching Young Children Mathematics*. Westport, CT: Praeger.

In this book Sydney Schwartz explains the importance of adopting a scientific approach to the teaching and learning of mathematics. He argues that as children learn to observe, compare and classify their knowledge they develop a deeper understanding of mathematical concepts.

Index